SalonOvations'
Day Spa
Operations

Delmar Publishers' Online Services

To access Delmar on the World Wide Web, point your browser to: **http://www.delmar.com/delmar.html**

To access through Gopher: **gopher://gopher.delmar.com**

(Delmar Online is part of "thomson.com", an Internet site with information on more than 30 publishers
of the International Thomson Publishing organization.)

For information on our products and services:

email: info@delmar.com   or   call **800-347-7707**

SalonOvations' Day Spa Operations

by
Erica T. Miller

Africa • Australia • Canada • Denmark • Japan • Mexico • New Zealand • Philippines
Puerto Rico • Singapore • Spain • United Kingdom • United States

NOTICE TO THE READER

Cover Design: Suzanne McCarron
Cover Photo: Michael Dzaman

Milady Staff:
Publisher: Catherine Frangie
Acquisitions Editor: Marlene McHugh Pratt
Project Editor: Annette Downs Danaher
Production Manager: Brian Yacur
Art/Design Production Coordinator: Suzanne McCarron

Printed in the United States of America
    8   9   10   XXX   05   04

For more information, contact Milady, 3 Columbia Circle, PO Box 15015, Albany, NY 12212-0515; or find us on the World Wide Web at http://www.Milady.com

Library of Congress Cataloging-in-Publication Data

Miller, Erica T.
    SalonOvations' day spa operations / by Erica T. Miller.
       p.   cm.
    Includes bibliographical references and index.
    ISBN: 1-56253-255-3
    1. Beauty Shop—United States—Management. 2. Health Resorts—United States—Management. I. Title
TT965.M56   96-102229
646.7'27—dc20   CIP

Contents

Dedication

I would like to dedicate this book to a student of mine, Ms. Julie Knight, in hope that her story may serve as an inspiration to other young people considering a career in the beauty industry. But even more, I feel that her story is an inspiration to us all.

Julie, a vivacious young lady, had attended a number of my classes and was a student of my basic body massage class. We had neared the end of the week and one of the final assignments for all students in the class was to report on a specific body system and also the reasons why they chose to take the body massage course. The purpose of these oral reports was to help develop speaking abilities and confidence. In past classes Julie had been a hard worker, but I sensed something more in this class. I just didn't know what. During the course of her report on the nervous system, she began to discuss the value of massage in connection with it. It was then that her story came out.

As she talked about it, I started taking notes. She began with, "Massage gave me an alternative in order to live!" I asked her what she meant and she told us (keep in mind that the whole class was in on this discussion) about how her life had been one of too much money, drugs, alcohol, and frenzy. She explained that she and her mother had never really bonded when she was a child and that she had felt unwanted most of her life. At 18 she inherited a trust fund that kept her in the rat race of drugs and trying to buy friends. She soon realized that money couldn't buy everything, especially happiness. To do something, she chose to go to a spa, The Oaks at Ojai, where the massage therapist performed a wonderful massage that was later to change her life. "I knew I didn't want drugs, so I spent this week to dry out. I couldn't sleep so I got massage. Money could buy me touch… the touch I had never received."

As the years went by and the money began to dry up, she became suicidal and had no purpose. "At 27 I knew there was something better but I didn't know what until I went to the Vapor Caves in Glenwood Springs, Colorado. The massage therapist there helped me, and I realized that massage was something I could do that could do some good for someone without hurting myself. I can't afford another emotional hurt. That's when I discovered I could get out of this mess." Julie enrolled in cosmetology school at the Glenwood Beauty Academy where the owners and instructors encouraged and inspired her to become a massage therapist and esthetician. I saw a young lady with a powerful mission. Julie said one more thing. "I love massage. My mother taught me to think about being healthy. This led to massage. And now I can use massage to be able to touch and help somebody else. I also gain from that touch. My money's gone now and I'm happy. I feel at real peace to help somebody and lose myself. I decided to live rather than die."

Would you ever imagine that your facial, body massage, or any treatment for that matter could save someone's life? It can and it will.

And Julie, thank you for being so brave as to share this story so publically with the readers of this book. All the difficulties you suffered growing up will serve to benefit many others. And most of all now, Julie, you are on your way to a peaceful, soul-satisfying career. I wish you the greatest and best in all your endeavors, for you have proven that you can do and be all that you choose to. Keep it up!

Preface

To some extent, the reasons for writing this book are the same as my reasons for writing *Day Spa Techniques*. My backgound is the same and will be repeated here for readers who don't have both books. However, that doesn't explain why the business part of day spas wasn't just added into the other book as a chapter or two. It's really simple. I believe that you cannot succeed in this field without a strong business approach to everything you do. From choosing equipment and products to setting up your programs and maintaining ongoing controls, you must have a business head and a sense of diligence to make it work.

Because day spas are the hot topic today, consultants are suddenly everywhere. That doesn't mean they are all qualified to help you. Two friends of mine, Dr. Judith Singer and Patricia Monteson, owners of Health Fitness Dynamics in Pompano Beach, Florida, are, in my opinion, the foremost destination and resort spa consultants in America, and perhaps abroad as well. I know that as of a few years ago they had done more than $150 million dollars in spa consulting projects, and it must be even greater today. They are very professional, experienced, low key, and now somewhat guarded due to the onslaught of unqualified, self-delusional "spa consultants."

I now see the same trend in day spa consultants, the experts who have popped up after having a massage at a spa, or after working in one right after beauty school for six months. This is a dangerous trend, one that stands to hurt us all and the industry as a whole. I spend a lot of my time as a consultant, often helping a spa after it has had a terrible experience and lost a great deal of money. Although I cannot possibly know everything and certainly don't claim to, this book has been designed to give you some general basic business guidance. As with all of my materials, I encourage you to go out and seek more opinions before determining your own. I do encourage you to hire a qualified consultant as needed but to check the person out and compare with other opinions and ideas. Then you must also experience several day spas before starting your own. If it's really worthwhile and you're planning to invest a substantial amount of money, take your time. My hope is that this book will serve as a guide to help you with the basics, with some of the questions to ask, with insight to protect you, and with the inspiration to feel confident about what you're planning to do.

And finally, a last word on my approach to business and this book. I am generally known to be straight, "shoot from the hip" as a close friend always says, and truthful. I am perhaps less diplomatic than I could be, but at least you always know where you stand with me. I would like each of you embarking on an endeavor in this field to base your business on these two simple principles—honesty and integrity. The whole concept of *Day Spa Operations* is based on a nonhype, practical approach to this field. If you develop and position your business to give your clients more than you expect to recieve, I believe God will reward that with more than you'll ever need. I often say in my classes, "Give your clients a dollar and a half in service for a dollar in cash and you'll always succeed."

I've been in this industry for more than twenty-five years. My company, Correlations, Inc., is more than seventeen years old and I have the most wonderful clients and the greatest, most effective, most devoted staff in America! I feel that I have been very blessed in this career. I hope you are as fortunate. I have tried my best to give you the most practical, useful information possible in a short book, a book that has been nonexistent until now. But it's imperfect and I hope you will, in turn, share your experience with the book with me so that I can continue to improve it in the future.

Credits

Photography:
Mr. Bob Kryzak—American Video
137 Whispering Hills, Coppell, TX 75019, (214) 462-8809

Day Spa Photos:
With Class, A Day Spa—Lynn and Gerald Kirkpatrick, owners
621 B. Chase Dr., Tyler, TX 75701, (903) 581-1745

Spa Layouts:
Ms. Diana Drake—RBD Interiors
7127 Echo Bluff, Dallas, TX 75248, (214) 931-5742

Acknowledgments

I wonder how I could thank the whole industry for their contributions to this book. Even though this is a business book for day spas, it's really an amalgamation of a million experiences with my own salon and day spa clients all over the country. As such I owe a tremendous debt to the many clients of my company, Correlations, Inc., for their assistance, whether they are aware of it or not. Each and every issue covered in the book is based on actual real-life experiences. I'm sad to say that many clients didn't make it and won't have this resource to help, and yet they hopefully contributed to your success. Some clients are mentioned and some are not, but to all of you, thank you. And to my staff, you have my great appreciation for your support and carrying on during the crunch times. I sure do appreciate each of you.

This book was very labor intensive on many people's parts. The photography for both *Day Spa Techniques* and this book are all due to the fine talents of Mr. Bob Kryzak, my all-time favorite photographer and absolute best video producer, Americom Video, Dallas, Texas. Once again Bob, I thank you for your talents and vision and especially for your patience with me! Most of the photography was shot in my friend, client, and wonderful technical contributor's day spa. Lynn, you so graciously allowed our team and the readers to peek into your business. Allowing us to photograph your operation and then contributing so much valuable information is deeply appreciated. Lynn Kirkpatrick is the very talented owner of one of the most attractive and unique day spas in the country, With Class, A Day Spa, Tyler, Texas.

Do you know any interior designers who would give so much time and expertise to the point of offering layouts? To Diana Drake, owner of RBD Interiors, Dallas, Texas, I thank you so much! I particularly thank you for caring so much about this industry and always being there for information, and for the uncanny ability you have for really helping our clients on their level, not the interior designer level!

Ginny and Frank Burge, owners of Day Spa Beautique Salon, Houston, Texas, one of the finest examples of a day spa in the country, I thank you for being so willing to share so much with so many. You are always so generous with information that many other professionals would never share. I so appreciate you! And in that same vein, I thank my dear friend and day spa owner, Kathy Driscoll, The Spa At The Houstonian, Houston, Texas. Your input has been so valuable, your support has kept me forging ahead, and your great business mind has been a joy to pick for the world to share! You're incredible!

Out of the many questionnaires sent and telephone calls made, I'm pleased to have the opportunity to thank a very small select group of experts who were so willing to share with others. I never realized until this project how unusual your attitudes were! You're very special and I thank each of you so much for caring about the business and for your contributions, your thoughts, brochures, and other proprietary information. Tamara Friedman, owner of Tamara Institut de Beauté in Farmington Hills, Michigan, thank you for being so open and willing to share your wonderful packages and information. Thank you Annette Hanson, great educator and president of Atelier Esthetique, New York, the foremost day spa training facility on the East Coast. Annette, a cohort in day spa education, thank you so much for the photos, comments, and support on this book.

Thank you David Miller, my long-time friend, co-fighter for the cause of esthetics, and co-owner along with his lovely wife, Mary, of the wonderful Day Spa, David & Mary, Indianapolis. And may I also thank you David and Mary for having the creativity and professionalism to produce some of the finest pieces of literature this industry has ever seen! To Leah Kovitz, a consummate professional esthetician and person of incalculable integrity, owner of New Image by Leah, Tucson, Arizona, and inventor/developer of the world renowned Parisian Body Polish Treatment, I thank you so much for all your input! Your English is absolutely fine and your contributions are so appreciated. And in this group, I added a very special friend from the ranks of the big resort destination spas, Ms. Marguerite Rivel, spa director of the five-star, five-diamond resort, The Broadmoor, Colorado Springs. Marguerite, thank you so much for the information provided and for being such a great sounding board for so many things. What a sharp, creative person you are!

And now I want to thank my two business partners, best friends, and practically my family, Paula Dean-Ball and Andy Sears. I think it's safe to say that these books wouldn't have happened without you! Paula, besides being the true friend that you are to have put up with me as I stressed out working on this project, for encouraging by your positive comments, and also for helping me so much to stay on track. Your brilliant comments and your ability to pick up those little vital points on the chapters as they evolved really polished the book! You were so appreciated. But most of all, knowing that my best friend was there to believe in it and support me made this such a lasting worthwhile project to do. And to you, Andy, also my friend, partner, contributor, so much of this we did together (more than you'll ever know). In addition to all the technical assistance provided on the equipment, your general pointers really helped the book come together. As for real life, I could leave it to write because I knew you were there holding the fort and what a fine job you did, too. I'll bet you can hardly wait till I do this again! Thank you both for your immeasurable contributions!

I cannot close without my thanks to the reviewers without whom there would be many holes and information missing. And last, but by far not least my thanks and appreciation really goes to all of you at Milady Publishing Company for being such a cohesive, cooperative team to work with. You each have made it a pleasure, not a nightmare! Marlene Pratt, my acquisitions editor, who is always so supportive and encouraging; the incredibly talented Annette Downs Danaher (I still can't believe you're so young!) who made me do it right; my dancing production manager, Brian Yacur; and for the great leadership and support of the publisher, Cathy Frangie. I thank each of you so much. And to your boss, President Nancy Roberson for being so smart to have you on staff! Thank you for all your talents, hard work, and excitement for this project!

Introduction

This book has been nearly two years in the making, from concept and research to the final writing. I have chosen the issues and concerns, each and every one of them from actual experiences. These experiences come from projects where I've been hired as the professional consultant, instances as a technical educator, and to a very large measure from the practical field experiences with my salon and day spa clients over a period of nearly twenty-five years. Although I speak to some issues also as a day spa owner, most of the concerns covered in this book have been very real problems that have caused real businesses I've dealt with to be less than they could be and, in some cases, actually fail. There is no way a business book on day spas can address all aspects of the business. The goal of this presentation has been to bring you to an awareness of as many core subjects as possible. There's not a heading or category in this book that couldn't be expanded, or even be a book by itself. Your mandate from me now is to read it, read it again, and then go out there and some more research.

There's no question in my mind that I've forgotten other things that are important. I don't begin to claim that this book is perfect. It never will be. But it's a start and I feel confident that the information will at least prevent some very costly mistakes. And at the last, I hope that from your study of this book you will gain a love and excitement for this business that those of us in it already have. It really does get in your blood! Personally, I know I've grown tremendously just from the challenge of writing it.

Why is there a need for a book on the business of a day spa? The question seems irrelevant at first, and then upon further thought it's very clear that there needs to be a book on the business side of day spa development. *Day Spa Techniques* is the book you will want to refer to in order to learn more about water, seaweed, or how to wrap a client after a mud application. But this is the book you need to make it all go together and to be successful.

You see, there are really two sides to the beauty business in America today. Some refer to it in a similar manner as right and left brain thinking—the very knowledgeable and talented technician personality and, conversely, the business personality. In general, the excellent outstanding technician is not necessarily a good businessperson, and vice versa. The businessperson doesn't really understand the depth of client care and treatments. If the operation has the wherewithal to operate with two different people for each side of the business, great. However, this isn't often the case. What is more likely is one person trying to do both sides. And even if there are two, what happens when one leaves the business?

In America today, an average of one out of every two salons that opens closes in less than one year. Is this statistic true? It unfortunately is! Why does this happen? Is it because the technician personality is trying to be the business personality, too, but just doesn't know what to do and often doesn't have the time to worry about it? Can a great technician become a good businessperson? It's difficult but possible, and that's the basis of this book.

There's another very important reason for this book. Today, business is tough and competition is getting stronger. To succeed in a day spa business requires a keen mind for trends and understanding consumer needs as the media does a better and better job of educating the public. That education isn't always accurate, which can make retraining a client a more challenging issue.

Americans are becoming very streetwise when it comes to health and beauty aids, salon services, spas, and the like. It's the job of the professional to stay on top of market developments and hopefully on the cutting edge of technology at all times. This requires a good business look at what's going on out there. Technicians who haven't been going to seminars and reading books and magazines in the past three to five years are antiquated in this author's opinion. The technology of skin and body care is moving forward at such a great pace that the intelligent day spa owner is in a constant search for knowledge.

So, from a business standpoint, what is a day spa? It's the 1990s salon! If you are planning to open a salon and don't consider and plan for day spa services, you've antiquated yourself before you've even started.

The final critical point in understanding the day spa from a business standpoint is making it work. You can spend half a million dollars opening a gorgeous day spa, but that doesn't guarantee success. You have to market the spa or it won't work. No matter how great a facial or body treatment you give, that doesn't guarantee success. The business has to be nurtured just like a child is nurtured by a parent. The better the upbringing, the better the chance for success. And just like in parenting, you must love your business and truly care about it.

Without a doubt, the day spa is the salon of the nineties and what a great opportunity it is indeed. Use this book as a foundation and keep growing. Good luck in the day spa business!

— Erica Miller

CHAPTER 1
The Day Spa Client

OVERVIEW

Day spas originate from destination spas where a person would go for a week to either lose weight, redefine a lifestyle, get in better shape, or just escape the stress of modern American life. The idea of a destination spa here in America really began in Europe. The word *spa* comes from the name of a hot springs village in Belgium called Spau. The European concept, however, was more "cure" oriented, that of staying for a week to correct health problems or ailments. The idea of a spa was not a vacation per se, but a place to go "take the waters" where the mineral waters would help alleviate specific problems. These *kur* towns as they are called are supported in many countries by the federal government and private industry. As an example, it's very common in Germany for a company to send an employee for a *kur* at the company's expense.

As the concept of a spa came to America, the idea evolved differently. Americans were and are more fitness oriented. Interestingly enough the first spas in America were often called "fat farms" because the primary goal of a week's stay was to eat slim and exercise. But the idea took off, spa attendance began to grow, and hundreds of destination spas popped up around the country. However, with the busy lifestyles of many men and women, taking a week off to sequester oneself in a spa environment was impossible, hence the birth of the day spa.

THE DAY SPA

Perhaps the first salon called a day spa was the brainchild of a yearly spa goer, Noelle De Caprio. She created a mini-version of the spa experience by way of beauty treatments. That was in 1974, and the day spa concept has now taken off nationwide. Today, of course, the day spa is often nearly as sophisticated as a destination spa without the hotel, food, and exercise facilities.

More detailed history and definition may be found in the book *Day Spa Techniques*, but suffice it to say that a day spa of today must have two elements to really make it a day spa. It must have some type of water therapy even if only a shower, and it must offer body treatments. And although water therapies make the day spa more akin to the European counterpart, it's the addition of body treatments that really clicks with the American consumer in the day spa today. A day spa should allow you to partake in most of what a destination spa offers but on a one-day or less basis. It's obviously difficult to offer everything, specifically the outdoor walking tracts, exercise equipment, sports, and swimming pool, not only from an investment standpoint

"Day spas will evolve into more specialized areas instead of just cloning the European spas of just pampering. They will have more 'how to' sessions with clients—nutrition, health, stress reduction, aquatic therapies, etc."—Lynn Kirkpatrick, With Class, A Day Spa, Tyler, Texas

1

"What a compliment it is to be in the industry we're in. People are giving us permission to touch them...that's the highest compliment."—Lynn Kirkpatrick, With Class, A Day Spa, Tyler, Texas

but also from the space required. The American consumer doesn't normally expect a day spa to offer sports and exercise facilities anyway.

So the day spa basically has evolved into a one-day facility for all the face and body care elements, primarily from a health preservation and beautification aspect. It's important to note here that due to the modernization and computerization of our society, touch is getting farther and farther away from us. As we grow more stressed and rush to keep up with life today, the need for what a day spa offers will continue to grow. And many busy people who have the disposable income to take spa vacations often lack the time, hence another reason for the validity of the day spa. Most day spas logically evolve from the traditional beauty salon (hair salon).

It's interesting to note the evolution in salon terminology. In the 1950s, we often referred to the facility as the "beauty parlor," in the 1960s and 1970s "beauty salon," in the 1980s "full service salon," and now "day spa." The emphasis, however, is away from hair services as the central theme of the operation, instead leaning much more toward facials and body care. You know beauty parlors and barber shops offered facials way back in the 1940s and 1950s, and full service salons offered all the chemical work and facials too. And now the day spa has gone way beyond all that to a complete person consciousness—full-body treatment.

. . . .

SPA POINT

The day spa is the salon of the 1990s, and planning related to opening a salon should include future growth with day spa concepts in mind. Without some form of day spa services, the salon is antiquated before it gets off the ground. The day spa client is looking for touch, rest, relief from stress, and improvement of health and well-being but within a limited amount of time. Therefore, the day spa is perfectly suited to the future American lifestyle.

. . . .

HEALTH AND BEAUTY TRENDS OF THE NINETIES AND BEYOND

"Day spas are the evolution of the fitness spa/destination spas and resorts for the I want it now and haven't got time society."—Lynn Kirkpatrick, With Class, A Day Spa, Tyler, Texas

Natural healing and home cures basically drifted into oblivion in the late 1800s due to the advent and development of modern medicine. Everyone grew up with some of grandmother's home cures for various ailments and problems, but the incredible development of medicine in this century has virtually blanketed the world. However, at the same time, this magnificent machine has also taken control of health care in America today. It's a massive, well-controlled money and power business. There is nothing particularly wrong with modern science and medicine. However, there is also nothing wrong with combining the best of the medical world with the best of the holistic world.

Probably the biggest deficit of modern medicine is that it seems to concentrate more on the symptoms and curing specific problems than looking at the whole individual from a preventative standpoint. The American consumer today is conscious of this and is searching for alternative avenues to good health. In the overall repertoire of holistic health care comes fitness and exercise of course, along with nutritional therapy and vitamin supplements because our food often no longer contains the nutrition it once had. And perhaps the spa, destination and day spa, is another powerful tool in preventative health care.

Burton Goldberg stated in the preface to *Alternative Medicine, The Definitive Guide* (compiled by The Burton Goldberg Group):

> ...I'm not against mainstream, conventional medicine. The Chinese have a saying about the wisdom of "walking on both feet," which means using the best of Eastern and Western procedures. That's what I want to see us do. There is no single approach that works for all people, or with all conditions. This goes for alternative medicine as well.
>
> Experience shows that you're likely to get the best results with a practitioner who has trained in a number of different modalities. There may be underlying factors influencing your health—nutritional deficiency, poor digestion, toxicity from environmental pollutants, or mental and emotional stress.
>
> You want a practitioner who is capable of determining exactly what needs to be done to help you regain health and vitality. You also want an open-minded practitioner who treats you as an individual. What's good for Harry is not necessarily good for Mary. You are biochemically unique.
>
> Here is a most important, optimistic, and totally realistic thought to carry with you. Most everything is reversible. You only need to find the right therapies. Be Well.

Impressive thoughts in an impressive book published in 1994 by Future Medicine Publishing, Inc. This book is more than one thousand pages in length and covers thousands of thoughts related to alternative medicine therapies, including many of the practices of spas. This book, by the way, is a consumer book and is sold in bookstores.

· ·

SPA POINT

The important point to be kept in mind here is that the American consumer is conscious of health and is searching for preventative good health alternatives. The "baby boomer" is aging. Health food specialty stores are evolving into full-blown grocery stores; exercise classes, in-home exercise equipment, and exercise video sales are at an all-time high. The day spa speaks perfectly to the consumer need for better health and well-being.

· ·

FIGURE 1-1 *Brochure from David & Mary, Indianapolis.*

WHO IS THE DAY SPA CLIENT?

Anyone seeking to take better care of himself/herself is a day spa client (Figure 1-1). To be more specific, a number of categories can be considered. At the same time, statistics point strongly to the fact that more than half the American population will reach the age of 50 by the year 2000. This aging population is looking to improve their appearance and preserve their health. Any combination of spa services may be popular in any given market, but a few typical suggestions will be given under each category. These categories are segmented for general reference purposes only and are not discriminatory in nature.

Luxury Class: Mr. or Ms. Too Much Money

Traditionally, women and men of wealth and leisure have frequented European and destination spas. The person in this category appreciates being cared for and pampered. Services for this client should concentrate on luxury, the best and most sophisticated of services. This client is demanding and well experienced and expects the best of all the treatments. This client is labor intensive but appreciates the best, most deluxe treatments available.

The top full-day package is often chosen. Equipment, service menus, and employee handling require a high degree of finesse. This client, however, may also be fickle and be a "spa hopper," the person never satisfied with any location who wants to visit many spas and experience many programs. This adds to the level of difficulty as the spa will always be compared with another facility.

Upper Middle Class Career Person: Mr. or Ms. Professional

This is probably the largest segment of spa and day spa visitors. Good health and well-being are important to this person. Career is very important and to function at top speed requires attention to self-care. This client, once introduced to spa services, is normally quite loyal and obedient. This person is intelligent and knowledgeable to some extent about beauty and health practices. A full complement of spa services is recommended for optimum client retention. This client will leave for a more fully equipped system if you're not on top of services and product trends. The most difficult aspect of caring for this client is the lack of available time for treatment, not a lack of money. Compact packages that get the client in and out quickly are most appreciated. A facial, body massage, and manicure package is always popular.

Hydrotherapy tub and massage combinations work well along with spot treatments for cellulite (in the case of women). This client appreciates your determination to grow and learn and will grow and learn right along with you. The sophisticated and technical facility will easily attract this client. Today, this is probably the largest segment of the day spa user population and should continue to grow well.

"As life becomes more hectic, the idea of an urban or suburban oasis for refreshing and rejuvenating will only grow. Consumers may have the resources to travel to destination spas/resorts, but not the time, so the day spa will continue to fit an important need."—Leah Kovitz, New Image By Leah, Tucson, Arizona

Average Middle Class Career Person: Mr. or Ms. Hard Worker

This client is ideally suited to the more middle-of-the-road day spa. Going to the extent of putting in all hydrotherapy equipment and tubs is not required by this client. This client is appreciative, quite loyal, and very willing to grow with you. This client appreciates savings on multiple purchases, frequent visits, and recommending future business. This client category will grow as public awareness expands and the number of day spas grows. This is the client desirous of visiting destination spas but without the time and financial wherewithal to do it regularly. Receiving a few services along with regular haircuts and facial treatments will automatically serve to grow the client and the range of this level of business. Generally don't expect this client to be a full-day or multiple-package person. Smaller, more economical packages suit this client. A good combination might be a facial/makeup duo or a hydrotherapy bath with a 30-minute massage.

"The Day Spa concept is a combination of health and pampering treatments.... The overall most important concept of the day spa is to pamper the clients and make them feel like the most important person there at all times."—Kathy Driscoll, The Spa At The Houstonian, Houston, Texas

Nonworking Parent Raising Children: Mr. or Ms. Stressed

This is the client who desperately needs a day spa for an escape. However it's quite difficult to get this client into the spa. Specific packages and specials should be offered to this group because they will not only revive as a result of the services but will also talk to everyone else in the PTA and neighborhood. This category of client is often the "alone" part of the average and upper middle class client. This client, male or female, has made the deliberate (assumably) choice to concentrate on parenting as a career. This is a determined class of client and will be fiercely loyal once you get him or her into the spa a time or two. Specials and packages are a must for this client, concentrating heavily on body massage and spot treatments for areas such as cellulite and bust.

Senior Citizens: Mr. or Ms. It's Too Late For Me

This client needs spa services. It won't make Mr. 75-years-old a 40-year-old puppy again, but improvement of skin and well-being is dramatic. This client is very difficult to obtain. Cajoling, education, and continual convincing are required to get this client in the spa. Try begging if necessary.

The reality is that this client can benefit from spa services in a major way, not only from tremendous skin improvement but also the natural improvement in well-being, reduction of aches and pains, and just better health. This client does well with water therapies, spot treatments for sore muscles and achy joints. Due to senior age, be cautious with health conditions and treatment contraindications. Good combinations include any hydrotherapy treatment with a body massage or facial. A manicure/pedicure combination with paraffin is also popular. This class of client is growing rapidly and couldn't need a spa more. If your choice is to concentrate on this group, have patience and consciously design programs around the conservative, frugal-minded person. Extra fluff is not necessary for this group as a whole. Although it may be the "fluff" that initially attracts them.

Teenagers: Mr. or Ms. I'm an Adult, Thank You

Teenagers certainly need some of the spa services, particularly in the area of oily/acne skin treatments, whether for the face only or back as well. Teens are busy, stressed-out people, and for the most part couldn't be less interested, unless of course, the skin is a wreck. This group is a bit fickle and unreliable. They want instant cures for acne and perfect bodies in one treatment. Due to traditional medical approaches to skin problems and teenagers, you can achieve great success if you can get to them.

Getting teenagers in and keeping them coming back is a bit of a challenge, but word spreads wildly and a teenage business can build rapidly with a few successes. The day before the prom they may be interested in pampering and luxuriating, but on a regular basis, in-depth and sophisticated services are "wasted on the young" who don't show much interest. A full complement of equipment is not particularly necessary for this group.

Children: Oops, I'm Too Young

One of the reasons many Europeans have a better consciousness of skin is because they were taught to take care of their skin from a young age. Dr. Albert Kligman, one of the original developers of Retin A and other acne treatment concepts, has been quoted as saying that the skin begins to age at 12 years old. If this is true, then shouldn't prepubescent children be learning skin care at that age or sooner? Although a child doesn't need the treatments adults do, periodic facials and body work are advisable from a maintenance point of view as well as from an educational standpoint. The treatments should be kept simple and easy for the child to understand. It's much better to instill a consciousness of beauty and health practices younger, not to mention creating your future business market.

. . . .

SPA POINT

It's important to clearly understand the seven different types of clients. The development and growth of your day spa will become highly dependent on which category(s) you choose to target as your audience. Even if you serve multiple categories overall, marketing techniques later will more easily segment if you clearly define to whom you're attempting to market.

. . . .

THE ISSUE OF MALE AND FEMALE

Male and female issues were deliberately not addressed previously. There are, however, issues that must be considered when planning to offer day spa services on the opposite sex, that is, female massage therapist giving a massage to a male, and vice versa. You must check with your local and state authorities regarding licensure requirements and limitations. This holds true about everything, but particularly in regard to the performance of services on the opposite sex. You may want to establish your own day spa policy regarding this. If you feel comfortable working on the opposite sex, great. If not, don't. If you want only males working on males, that's fine too. But keep in mind that this can be a booking nightmare if your only male technician is off the day you want to book a male client.

It's just plain good sense to be careful about booking strangers or persons with obvious alternative motives. And it's advisable that another staff member be on site somewhere, though not in the treatment room, when body services are being done.

Developing your spa around the fact that your client base is male or female is an option, but consider it well. Most day spas today are being developed and designed in a unisex style. Soft pink everything may be nice for a female clientele but it will absolutely kill a male clientele. Try brown and watch the opposite happen. A word about the male versus female client. It is this author's belief that the male client base will continue to grow at a steady pace. Women tend to be more fickle and try other places and products. You will have a more loyal client in a male and once he's convinced of the validity of what you're selling him, he will do what you say, if you're truthful and don't oversell him. You will also learn that men are drawn more easily to some services than women and vice versa. A body massage is always very appealing to a male and is a good business draw. A cellulite reduction treatment will be an instant draw to a woman.

> *"A day spa is a respite from stress for active professionals who are not able to leave their workplace for days at a time. It can also be a place to escape for a day or for just anyone who needs escape."*
> —*Marguerite Rivel, Spa Director, The Broadmoor, Colorado Springs*

. . . .

SPA POINT

Consideration of gender needs is important in the development of your day spa decor, programs, staffing, and promotions.

. . . .

THE CLIENT BASE

Day spa treatments are really for everyone, no matter what age, sex, or income level. However, at the time of this writing, it is, perhaps, more realistic to base the premise of this book on the current fact that facial and body care is of the greatest interest and within reach of the middle class and above. Eventually, day spa services will transcend all groups, but due to the newness and the educational awareness of what spa treatments can do, the person planning to open a day spa at this time would do well to base the planning and targets on the upper three markets mentioned previously. As such, most of the work in this text will be based on the premise of three markets.

The Luxury Market

This encompasses the more well-to-do client accustomed to linen and lace, if you will. This market will necessarily require all possible services in a luxurious atmosphere. Attention to openness and large space, decor, and quality of furnishings will be important. The client will expect great detail in service and presentation. A day spa servicing this client group will probably be larger and more extravagant. High-end products and services will be suitable to this market.

The Upper Middle Market

This is your high-end upper management group. People in this group will want quality and presentation as well but will want the emphasis placed more on effectiveness than pampering. Treatments still must pamper and be elegant but not to the extent of the luxury market. Large space is not as critical in this market. Products must also be upscale and results oriented. This day spa will offer a good complement of services and packages but perhaps not to the extent of the luxury market.

The Middle Market

As stated earlier, this is your middle class career person who understands and needs to pay attention to health and good grooming. This day spa will be more practical and doesn't require the opulence of the other two. Services will lean toward the more basic but still be full body oriented. Decor and presentation need not be extravagant as this group is results oriented and not as concerned with the presentation. This category will be large and often cross over into upper middle. The danger in this category is to become too basic. Presentation and quality are still important criteria.

· ·

SPA POINT

The three categories, luxury, upper middle, and middle, may seem to be very segregated but in reality they are not. As you will learn in chapter 6, the design and development of the spa may overlap or differentiate as much as you like. A luxury spa doesn't necessarily mean large. However, a 7' x 9' facial room isn't appropriate for this market either. Throughout the book, the three separations are developed to assist you in planning your market and budget. These classifications are merely a basic, simple way to give you some optional directions. They will overlap greatly in that day spas are overall upscale in nature. So another way to break them up in your mind might be by investment range, from smaller, medium, to larger in scope and construction.

· ·

Synopsis

Day spas are not only the buzzword for the remainder of this century. In the opinion of this author, the development and growth of the day spa market will serve to change the professional beauty industry forever. With the peak income-producing years of baby boomers occurring during this time, the progressive service-minded professional will find that offering day spa services is an absolute must ... not an option. So why not begin today?

Review

1. How did the term *day spa* come about?

2. What are the two most important factors making a salon a true day spa?

3. What type of client base would you like to concentrate on and why?

CHAPTER 2
The Day Spa Home

OVERVIEW

If we wanted to shorten this chapter to one sentence or less to discuss where a day spa is appropriate, the answer would probably be anywhere, because that's how strong the day spa concept is. However, it's obviously not quite that simple. Keeping in mind that a day spa is really a salon with body and water treatment features, you'll find that it lends itself to almost anywhere you would want a beauty or health facility.

REGULATIONS

When considering the day spa home, the first and most critical things to investigate are the local, state, and/or federal regulations related to opening a day spa. Due to the fact that the day spa is primarily a salon-type facility, the first phone call you might make or letter you write should be to the state board of cosmetology. You must know what the regulations are in your state and local areas.

Massage and body treatments in many states are not under the state board of cosmetology, but rather the Department of Health. Some states lack state regulations but have city or local requirements. If your State Board of Cosmetology can't give you detailed requirements, also contact the Department of Health in your state and explain what you are planning to do.

If you will be doing construction, you will additionally need to check into local regulations and requirements for building permits and inspections for construction, plumbing, and electrical needs. It is strongly recommended that all regulatory bodies be consulted well in advance of any construction you plan to do. Many a salon and day spa have been shut down before opening due to a violation of regulations that could easily have been followed. So be sure to check into that during your thinking stages. Don't wait until the last minute. Late problems can cause expensive mistakes.

. . . .

SPA POINT
Adhering to local, state, and federal regulations from the beginning can save you time, money, and heartache later.

. . . .

WHERE IS A DAY SPA IDEALLY SUITED?

Traditional Full Service Salon

As previously stated, the traditional full service salon is the most likely placement for a day spa. Full service in this case means a salon offering hair, esthetic, makeup, and nail care services. To convert this operation into a day spa requires the addition of services and hopefully space. If the salon is constructed in such a way that water facilities and massage room additions are not possible, the salon will be severely limited in the body treatment options open to it, and although some body treatments can be done in the facial room, it wouldn't really be fair to officially categorize it as a day spa. It is the opinion of this author that at the very minimum a day spa should have shower facilities. If the salon has no shower or other hydrotherapy services, perhaps a better term for this type of facility might be *dry spa* indicating that body services are being done but not taking away from the true day spa that invests in hydrotherapy facilities.

If the salon can expand and gain space, the ideal conversion to a day spa would be to add a shower and/or wet room and massage room. A wet room is a room constructed with either tile or some other waterproof substance, a drain in the floor, and shower hose or other hydrotherapy device. The room should be large enough to have a bed where a technician can perform treatments on the client. It's also recommended to have another dry room for massage; thus both rooms can be used simultaneously and intermixed depending on treatments. If space doesn't allow for both, keep in mind that treatments can be done in the wet room. If you're building a salon with plans for hydrotherapy in the future but are not ready to implement it as yet, build the room of waterproof material with a drain in the floor and then just cover the floor with a carpet until you're ready to implement. Many salons use additional wet rooms as wax or makeup rooms until the need arises for body treatment rooms.

"In a society of technology, the lack of communication and touch has been lost (computers, phone mail, ATMs, etc.). Now the day spa is giving the client the personal attention thus removing stress in their lives."—Ginny Burge, Day Spa Beautique Salon, Houston, Texas

Esthetic Salon

In most cases the esthetic salon is already fairly well geared to day spa conversion, but the addition of water facilities and treatment rooms would be the same as for the full service salon. Many esthetic salons have very little space. Even just the addition of a shower onto the existing treatment room can serve to make a viable conversion.

Electrolysis Clinic

Many electrologists don't realize that they are often sitting on a day spa. Water source and treatment table is a common denominator for both, and if the space is there an electrolysis clinic can easily become a day spa as well. There is a natural affinity for esthetic services when electrolysis is being done. If the client cares enough to have permanent hair removal done, he/she is also a good candidate for esthetic and day spa services. If the electrolysis clinic is equipped in a manner similar to a physician's office and has many small rooms, it may be easy to convert one or two rooms into a wet area and treatment center for the body.

Medical Facility

Rapidly becoming a commonplace occurrence, dermatologists' and plastic surgeons' offices are opening day spa facilities on site. As the 1990s proceed into the next century, the advent of day spa doctors' offices will naturally grow. Additionally, hospitals, clinics, and rehabilitation centers will become day spa operations as well.

The goal of treatment in medical and medically related facilities may lean more toward the curative, remedial side of beauty but certainly they offer a myriad of strictly beauty-related programs and services as well. Regulations and requirements for day spa facilities as related to a medical practice will vary from state to state. It is imperative that the physician-owner be aware of the balance between medical and beauty-related goals.

Body Massage Center

The body massage center is a natural, in the same manner as the electrolysis clinic. Bringing water into a massage center is sometimes a problem if the facility was not designed with the need for water in mind. If the facility has water, it's quite easy to convert a couple of rooms into day spa treatment rooms.

Hotels

Many of the more upscale hotels already have spa facilities (Figures 2-1, 2-2). Just as the addition of exercise facilities became the byword of the 1980s, the 1990s requirement will be day spa facilities. The day spa facility in the hotel may be operated under the ownership of the hotel or as a concession, completely independent of the hotel other than mutual promotion

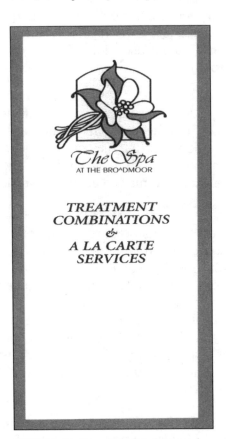

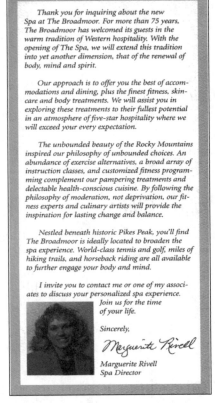

Thank you for inquiring about the new Spa at The Broadmoor. For more than 75 years, The Broadmoor has welcomed its guests in the warm tradition of Western hospitality. With the opening of The Spa, we will extend this tradition into yet another dimension, that of the renewal of body, mind and spirit.

Our approach is to offer you the best of accommodations and dining, plus the finest fitness, skincare and body treatments. We will assist you in exploring these treatments to their fullest potential in an atmosphere of five-star hospitality where we will exceed your every expectation.

The unbounded beauty of the Rocky Mountains inspired our philosophy of unbounded choices. An abundance of exercise alternatives, a broad array of instruction classes, and customized fitness programming complement our pampering treatments and delectable health-conscious cuisine. By following the philosophy of moderation, not deprivation, our fitness experts and culinary artists will provide the inspiration for lasting change and balance.

Nestled beneath historic Pikes Peak, you'll find The Broadmoor is ideally located to broaden the spa experience. World-class tennis and golf, miles of hiking trails, and horseback riding are all available to further engage your body and mind.

I invite you to contact me or one of my associates to discuss your personalized spa experience. Join us for the time of your life.

Sincerely,

Marguerite Rivell

Marguerite Rivell
Spa Director

FIGURE 2-1 *Several upscale hotels and resorts, such as The Broadmoor in Colorado Springs, offer guest spa facilities.*

FIGURE 2-2 *Consider how an upscale hotel can be enhanced by spa facilities.*

The Spa
at the Houstonian

Fax machines, portable phones.
Reading the headlines on the way to work.
More to accomplish, less time to do it in.
City dwellers in the '90s have certainly redefined stress!

Stress, in controlled, managed increments can be a healthy stimulus that propels us toward growth and excellence. Conversely, stress that we have little or no control over can assault our senses and slowly rob us of our peace of mind. Stress that slowly accumulates and remains unchecked can become a detriment to your health.

True health is preventive in nature and requires that wellness become a daily goal. Ignoring the signals and delaying the solutions can keep you trapped in an unhealthy phase of your life. With mounting deadlines and pressures, it becomes so easy to eat for convenience rather than nutrition and to react to situations rather than resolve them.

The spa acknowledges that busy people need effective solutions as they attempt to combat the effects of stress and enhance the quality of their lives. We offer services that are designed to be a healthy component to any wellness program. We encourage you to explore the many options available to you. We suggest that time taken for you, to recharge, is not a self-indulgent luxury. It is a truly a necessary tool that can help safeguard your greatest treasure, your Health.

The Spa at the Houstonian · 111 N. Post Oak Lane · (713) 680-0626

FIGURE 2-3 *Hotels and spas should promote their services together. Guests will be attracted to the conveniences and luxury of both facilities.*

(Figure 2-3). This category will continue to grow and expand in order to compete with destination spas.

Health Clubs/ Fitness Centers

This is another natural blend. Health clubs and fitness centers cater to the person who cares to look and feel good. It is an ideal facility for the inclusion of a day spa. Additionally, because the member attends the facility multiple times during the week, this makes it even more conducive to programs based upon a series of multiple treatments to achieve a result. This category will grow dramatically for the baby boomers who increase their health consciousness and become aware of their aging appearance as well.

Retirement Centers

This category does not refer to a nursing home or invalid facility. The effective day spa can elegantly be a part of an exclusive retirement community facility. These facilities are normally upscale and cater to the upper middle income to wealthy client, thus rendering it an ideal facility for day spa services. Hydrotherapy and massage services will be very popular as the baby boomer ages and realizes there is comfort and relief of aches and pains.

Community Centers and Social Clubs

Although a rather uncommon area for day spa development, some communities are banding multiple service facilities together for the benefit of the public. The YMCA, Junior League, country clubs, and certain social clubs show great interest in having day spa services on a private membership basis. This category can be very limited, hence risky, unless the size, affluence, and client interest are extensive.

. . . .

SPA POINT

The most important factor in determining a home for a day spa lies in the demographics of the potential clientele. Anywhere can become a day spa if all the factors are solid. The typical salon is certainly the most likely place for a day spa while the community center is probably the least. But the final choice depends on you, your goals, your target clientele, and all the other normal business factors in determining a location for your business.

. . . .

Synopsis

A day spa is suited to any professional environment where professional services are being offered, but perhaps the most ideal environment is the current full service salon if, in fact, it is full service. Conversion to a day spa is simpler in this environment. Day spas will be built without hair services, catering strictly to the skin, in medical practices, in chiropractic centers, in massage facilities, and the like, but the important point in determining where a day spa should be and how it's developed should be based upon research, demographic study, and market research.

Review

1. Why is a beauty salon suited for day spa development?

2. What makes an electrolysis clinic a good spot for a day spa?

3. Why would a fitness center be a good place to offer services that require a series or multiple treatments?

4. Can a retirement center really do well as a day spa?

CHAPTER 3
Developing Your Spa Program

OVERVIEW

In some respects, this may be the most important chapter in the book, because your final program will determine what your day spa will actually become. But at the same time, this chapter is also where the birth of your day spa will take place. Whether you're adding to an existing facility or starting from scratch, most of the same thought processes should take place. There are many important factors to consider before delving into the actual program. Without enough time and thoughtful research given many a day spa has failed. The most important thing to do is to take your time and research everything from all angles. Seek the advice of experts in the field also. It's sometimes advantageous to hire a professional consultant in advance of the project. But of course, choose your consultant carefully.

PREPROGRAM DEVELOPMENT

Target Market

The demographics of your market will be valuable in developing your client base. The seven types of client classifications from chapter 1 will represent part of your target market. Your target market will be the group or groups for whom you plan to build your program. It's very important to have a clear idea of the group to which you want to market your services and products. From the time you graduate from beauty school to the day you open your own day spa, you must be thinking about the client base you're building. For example, the type of customer that frequents K-Mart isn't the same person who frequents Neiman Marcus. There's not a thing wrong with K-Mart or Neiman Marcus. In fact, if you were offered one hundred shares of stock in either company as a free gift surely you wouldn't turn it down.

The point to keep in mind here is that the K-Mart client and the Neiman Marcus client are different, have different expectations, and want to visit a day spa that looks different. Do you have a preference of which client you'd like to cater to? Now you first may want to say, "Oh, the Neiman's client of course because she has more money," but think some more. Just because someone has money doesn't mean she'll spend it, or spend it easily. In some cases, the more affluent client may require more white glove care than the K-Mart client who is often readily pleased.

· ·

SPA POINT
The point here is slightly exaggerated but the reality is that different client groups relate differently to all aspects of the day spa from the decor to the pricing, types of products, packaging, service menu, and client care.

· ·

Research Competition

The next important consideration in preprogram development is to understand what you're up against. Have you researched your competition? Do you know area prices and general appearances? To what are the clients generally attracted? This is not to suggest that you should fear your competition. Quite the contrary. The reality is that the more spa services being offered in your community, the more the consumer demand will grow as well. People will jump on what they perceive to be the hot thing. But you must always stay on top of what's happening around you. You must be aware not only of other salons but also of what's happening in the cosmetic world outside, the department, grocery, and drug stores, right along with the direct sales cosmetic lines. Competition is healthy and helps the industry grow for everyone. Later when we discuss choosing product lines, you'll learn that having an "exclusive" may not always be the best thing.

Remember if you're the only one out there doing something, you have a harder row to hoe with the client educational process than if the client is hearing about a service everywhere.

Financial Analysis

You'll need to do a clear-cut financial analysis. Have you determined a budget from which to work? Do the rewards appear to outweigh the costs? Why do you want a day spa in the first place? What are your short-term and long-term goals for the day spa? How much money do you plan to spend? Will you finance it all yourself or obtain a loan from the bank? If you plan to obtain a loan you must be able to present a business plan to the bank. This business plan not only delineates in detail what you want to do, why, and how much it will cost, but should also show income projections for the next three to five years.

Whether you are borrowing money or not, you should force yourself to develop a business plan. By setting budgets and goals, you may save yourself from the disaster of running out of money in the middle of the project or even down the road during the actual running of the business. The business plan will also show you where your limitations will be, and then you can balance that with the demographics of your market, what you must have and what can wait, how much money you will have to live on until the clientele builds, and so forth.

It is suggested that you make a business plan even if the day spa development project is an add-on to an existing successful facility. There are always new challenges to calculate. Business plans will be discussed more fully in another chapter.

"Make sure you have enough money. You need enough money for one year of business without having to use your savings. Do not expect to make money on day 1!"—Annette Hanson, Atelier Esthetique, New York

Time Frame

What is your time frame for the development of your day spa? Are you allowing yourself plenty of time to research the project well before making final commitments to contractors and suppliers? This is a most important category of your preparatory work. Rushing into opening will negatively impact you from the very beginning. Don't embark on a project like this without really researching the industry. Get bids, talk to various suppliers and contractors. You can learn a wealth of information just from these discussions. And anyone balking or hesitant to share information with you should go on notice in the back of your mind.

Licensing Requirements

As stated earlier, you must investigate the licensing requirements of the state board of cosmetology or Department of Health. This will determine your employee needs as well.

. . . .

SPA POINT

Above all, taking a business approach, not a whimsical approach, to developing your day spa is critical to your success. A day spa's basic success potential can make it or break it at this point. Developing a day spa is serious business and requires detailed and careful planning.

. . . .

SPA SERVICES

Once the target market and budget has been relatively refined, the definition of the day spa programs can be developed. The selection of spa services will be geared to your market and budget. Also remember that in addition to determining the services, you must consider the overall mood and decor of the day spa. Services will be briefly discussed first by category, then a number of packages will be suggested.

Hair Services

Styling

Cutting

Highlighting and coloring

Perming

Hair conditioning

Scalp treatments

Nails

Regular manicures

Spa manicures (includes special exfoliation, specialized massages and masks for hands)

French manicures

Hot oil massages for hands/feet

Regular pedicure

Spa pedicure (includes special exfoliation, specialized massages and masks for feet)

Nail art (wraps, sculptures, appliques, etc.)

Facial Treatments

Basic deep cleansing facial treatment

Deluxe treatment (may include an enzyme or special exfoliation, ampoule, or super conditioner)

Specialized spa facial treatment (may include special exfoliation, mud or seaweed masks, layering treatments, etc.)

Makeup application

Makeup lesson

Facial waxing (eyebrows, lips, chin, sideburns, full face)

BODY TREATMENTS

In general most treatments could be performed in a dry room except hydrotherapy treatments, salt glows or body polishes, and mud masks. Some technicians will do these treatments in a dry room, but it must be remembered that the removals are difficult and extremely time-consuming. Exfoliations and muds are normally recommended for wet areas for simplicity and speed of removal. Therefore, the treatments being presented will be listed under the ideal treatment room situation first. Refer to *Day Spa Techniques* for detailed explanations for removal procedures in wet and dry rooms.

It should also be pointed out here that budget and space will determine to a great degree the number and variety of hydrotherapy equipment chosen for the day spa. If a wet room is available, be sure to install a regular hand-held shower system for body rinsing irrespective of whether you put in a Vichy shower or a hydrotherapy tub. This will allow more flexibility with the treatments as well.

"It's fun seeing people after they've had these treatments and seeing what a big difference it makes in their life!" —Ginny Burge, Day Spa Beautique Salon, Houston, Texas

Wet Room

HYDROTHERAPY

Shower (warm and/or cool showers)

Steam bath or room

Inhalation room (herbal, aromatherapy)

Swiss shower

Vichy shower (Figure 3-1)

Scotch hose (hydromassage)

Whirlpool (herbal, milk, mineral baths)

Hydrotherapy tub (Figure 3-2) (underwater hydromassage; herbal, milk, mineral, seaweed baths)

BODY TREATMENTS

Body exfoliation (salt glows, body polishes, enzyme peels)

Body masks (mud, seaweed, herbal, paraffin, parafango)

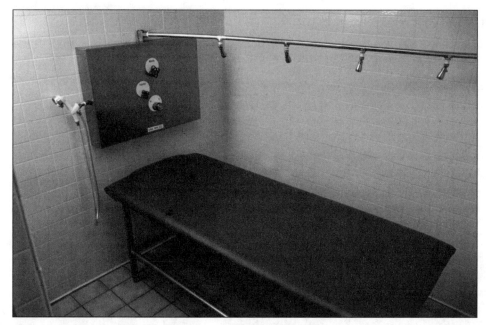

FIGURE 3-1 *The Vichy shower rains water from above, targeting specific parts of the body.*

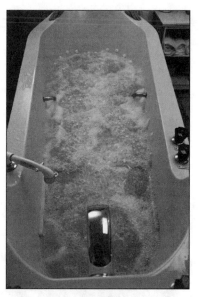

FIGURE 3-2 *The hydrotherapy tub provides clients with underwater hydromassage.*

Body wraps (herbal, seaweed)

Spot treatment wraps (bust, cellulite, back, arms and legs)

Body tanning (application of self-tanning solutions after exfoliation)

Dry Room

Body dry brushing

Body exfoliation (depending on product difficulty)

Body masks (seaweed, herbal, paraffin, parafango)

Body wraps (herbal, seaweed)

Spot treatments (bust, back, cellulite, arms and legs)

Body tanning

Body massage (numerous options from regular Swedish massage to Shiatsu, manual lymph drainage, deep tissue, and aromatherapy)

Dry sauna room/cabin

Thermal heat treatments (blankets, packs, etc.)

· ·

SPA POINT

The services you ultimately offer may depend on whether or not you have a wet room. Your marketability and flexibility expand greatly when you plan for a wet room from the beginning if at all possible.

· ·

SERVICES IN THE DAY SPA

As stated earlier, there are two basic requirements to consider your establishment a day spa—water and body treatments. Beyond that, a day spa can offer a multitude of services. The following provides a brief discussion of the various services you might consider.

Hair

If the spa is truly complete and has a full hair department, all cutting, color, and perm work will be offered as always (Figures 3-3, 3-4). A great new spa service for the hair department would be a spa scalp treatment, one that concentrates on the scalp itself, not so much on the hair. The spa scalp treatment may incorporate plants, aromatherapy, mud, or marine algae extracts in the form of massage and mask for the head.

FIGURE 3-3 Complete day spas will offer a wide range of services, including hair care and chemical treatments.

FIGURE 3-4 The decor of the hair care station should fit the image of the day spa.

Nails

Spa manicures and pedicures are becoming very popular and allow the nail technician to charge a higher price for the procedure (Figures 3-5, 3-6, 3-7). Spa manicures and pedicures involve some type of skin exfoliation, then foot and hand baths using "spa" products, followed by massage using essential oils or specially designed extracts beyond a normal massage lotion, and finally a special mud or seaweed mask for the arms/hands and legs/feet. The treatments can be simple or quite involved.

Facial Treatment

This area has been well developed and quite sophisticated for some time. (Figure 3-8) To develop specific spa-type treatments would normally involve the inclusion of muds, seaweeds, and aromatherapy into treatments in the form of masks or massages. Facial treatments can also be coordinated to do at the same time as some body treatments. It depends on the program development, timing, and expertise of the technician.

FIGURE 3-5 *Nail technicians have their own stations in the day spa.*

FIGURE 3-6 *Is your nail service prominently displayed?*

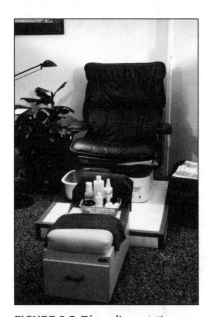

FIGURE 3-7 *The pedicure station should be comfortable for your client and should fit the image of the day spa.*

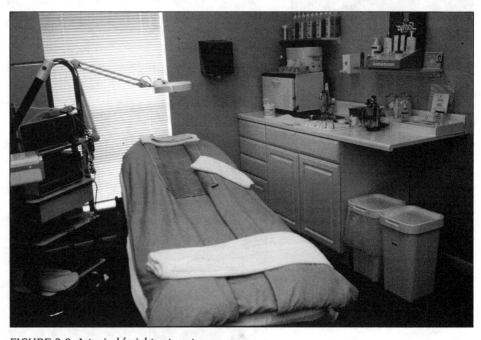

FIGURE 3-8 *A typical facial treatment room.*

Body Treatment

The hub of the true day spa, treatments for the body, can be as simple as a body massage to full body seaweed and mud wraps (Figure 3-9). With the benefit of combining hydrotherapy equipment and body treatments, service potential becomes virtually limitless.

Hydrotherapy

This is probably the area of greatest concern and cost in developing a day spa program. There are many different options available in this area, from as simple as a plain shower to the most sophisticated and expensive hydrotherapy tub. In the middle lie Vichy showers, Swiss showers, steam rooms or showers, saunas, whirlpools, and Scotch hose. What do these modalities offer?

FIGURE 3-9 *A body massage bed.*

SHOWER
For cleansing purposes prior to body treatment; facilitates removal of seaweeds and muds from masks and wraps; for relaxation and warming the body before massage.

SWISS SHOWER
Form of water massage from any number of jets or shower heads depending on the manufacturer; sprays water at strategically targeted areas to stimulate circulation and metabolism; often showers the client with pulsating sprays of warm to cold water for relaxation and invigoration.

VICHY SHOWER
A wonderful rain shower from above. Client reclines on bed and the shower heads rain on the client from a pole extending the length of the bed (Figure 3-10). Some Vichy showers have warm and cold pulsation capabilities as well. Also used for rinsing muds and seaweeds from the body.

SCOTCH HOSE
Somewhat like a firefighter's hose to target a spray of water at areas of the body to stimulate circulation and elimination of toxins. The spray is normally under high pressure and is applied to the client from a distance of 6–8 feet or more. The client holds onto handles extending from the wall for balance.

SAUNA
Dry heat cabinet designed to stimulate circulation and perspiration to eliminate toxins and invigorate the body.

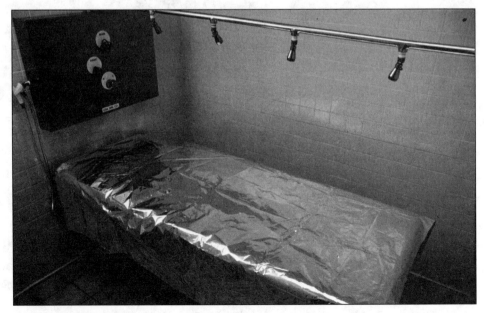

FIGURE 3-10 *The Vichy shower plays a variety of roles in the day spa, such as water therapy and rinsing muds and seaweeds from the body.*

STEAM SHOWER/CABINET

Moist heat by steaming. Often essential oils such as eucalyptus are infused to help with sinus and better breathing.

Designed also to stimulate, invigorate, and facilitate elimination of toxins.

INHALATION ROOM

Similar to the effect of a steam shower or cabinet but drier. The essences of aromatherapy oils are released through diffusers and are designed to help relieve congestion.

JACUZZI/WHIRLPOOL TUB

A tub aerated by air and/or water jets to stimulate bubbling of the water. Relaxes client and stimulates circulation. Often multiple people will use tub simultaneously.

HYDROTHERAPY TUB

A sophisticated tub with strategically located jets of both water and air, along with an air hose to provide for underwater massage of the client by the technician. Jets are controlled by technician to provide another form of water massage.

Seaweeds and essential oils can be included for a thalassotherapy treatment. *Thalassotherapy* means using seaweed and seawater extracts in treatment. This tub treatment is customized for the client and is done strictly individually.

TYPES OF BODY TREATMENTS TO OFFER

It will be helpful to do a brief description of the body treatments for clarity. However, to fully understand the techniques for performing any of these services, please refer to *Day Spa Techniques*. Now let's look into the treatments.

Body Exfoliation

The purpose of this is to smooth skin and remove dead scaly skin.

SALT GLOWS

These normally incorporate salts from mineral deposits, the Dead Sea, etc. Mix salts with a lotion or oil and massage over the body. This can be done quickly when done in conjunction with other combinations of treatments or slowly and more luxuriously when given as a treatment alone.

BODY POLISH

This incorporates ground pumice, nuts, pearls, or other substances dispersed in a cream format to remove dead skin and polish skin at the same time.

ENZYME PEEL

Enzyme peels incorporate substances such as papaya that will in essence chemically dissolve the dead cells without the surface active abrasiveness.

These are normally applied like a mask and allowed to sit for a while before being rubbed or washed off.

Body Masks

A great variety of body masks are available and their purpose varies greatly according to the mask chosen. As a general rule, body masks are designed to moisturize, tone, and help the body rid itself of wastes and toxins by stimulating the blood and lymph circulation. Certain types of masks are particularly popular in day spas, muds and seaweeds in particular. The uses listed would be for just applying the product and letting it sit on the skin for a specified amount of time. However, as the next section will delineate, wraps have added features to masking alone.

MUD
A number of muds and clays are used in masks today, but for body treatments the primary function is to soften and pull impurities out of the system. There are sea muds, clay muds, vegetable-based muds, mountain muds, and others. The study of mud is more fully covered in *Day Spa Techniques*.

SEAWEED
Seaweed is the most popularly used substance in spa treatments because of the high mineral content and the ability to improve the body's own metabolism.

HERBAL
These are masks made of various herbal extracts mixed into a paste and then painted on as a body mask.

PARAFFIN
Warmed paraffin is applied to the body and layered over skin covered with some nutritional product. The product is better absorbed by the skin due to the surface seal of the warm wax. The oils in the wax also soften and smooth the skin. Paraffin body masks are very popular in winter.

PARAFANGO
This is the best of both worlds—a combination of paraffin and mud. The mask coverage is like the normal paraffin seal and the mud provides the mineralization.

Body Wraps

There are actually two known types of body wrapping. In one the whole body is blanketed in plastic, foil, linen, or other cocoon-like wrap. In the other specific parts of the body are wrapped in plastic or similar substances.

This author does not believe in the individual constricting wraps. Full body wrapping is cozy and wonderful where tight partial wrapping may be too constrictive and dangerous. None of the wraps discussed here are of the constricting type. The purpose of the wrap is to seal the substances placed underneath as well as to promote heat, thereby increasing body circulation and product absorption along with elimination of toxins through perspiration. The process of perspiring and eliminating toxins is often called *detoxification.*

HERBAL
Herbal wraps are herbal-essence-saturated linen sheets. These sheets have been steeped and kept warm in a device called a hydroculator. The sheets are then wrapped around and over the client, followed by rubber sheets and blankets to keep the linen sheets warm as long as possible. The client is cocooned for about 30 minutes and comes out feeling refreshed and invigorated.

SEAWEED
Depending on the product supplier and directions, seaweed wraps may be done in either plastic or a type of Mylar foil. As a general rule, when Mylar foil is used there is greater heat transference and utilization. These are chosen when greater perspiration is desired such as in cellulite spot treatments. Where more product absorption and skin softening is desired, plastic may be more suitable. The wrap materials may intermix according to the individual client needs.

Spot Wraps

The wrapping concept and materials are the same as listed previously. The spot wraps basically treat only specified areas such as bust, cellulite, a sore muscle area, or lower back. Again, however, this is not a constricting wrap. Spot treatments are viable for 30-minute sessions and are repeated frequently. A cellulite treatment, for example, must be done quite often to achieve measurable effects. The goal in any spot treatment is to utilize ingredients, heat, and time to facilitate the relaxation of the muscle and dispersion of toxins as in cellulite, and to increase circulation to improve skin texture and nutrition.

Body Tanning

In this case body tanning does not mean tanning beds. This author is adamantly opposed to tanning beds and booths for the inherent risks involved and the fact that they are contrary to good skin care. However, the quality of self-tanners or auto bronzers has improved dramatically of late. The problem with these lotions and creams lies in the ability to apply them smoothly and evenly. It is far better to offer an exfoliation treatment followed by tanning application in the day spa rather than at home. The exfoliation removes the dead cells on which the lotion can accumulate. The application by a professional is much smoother, and the client then has to maintain at home what the day spa began and return periodically for a repeat treatment. Tanning should always be sold as polish and tan together, exfoliation and tanning combined. Don't separate if you want quality results. The combination should have one price.

. . . .

SPA POINT

A *good balance between hydrotherapy equipment, body, face, nails, and hair is important. If you plan to invest in a hydrotherapy tub or a Vichy shower, plan on using and marketing them as fully as possible.*

. . . .

DEVELOPMENT OF THE DAY SPA MENU

For every consultant and professional in the industry you will have a different view of how a menu should be developed. This will be a discussion of a number of ways in which a menu can be determined. The development of the menu shouldn't be rushed and all your demographic factors should be considered. Keep the following in mind at all times.

- What is your target market?

- Who are you trying to reach?

- What are your goals and what treatments do you really want to offer?

- What does your competition offer?

- Pricing will be affected by your client base, area, equipment and products, and competition.

The single most important thing to remember in the development of a menu is the quality of the literature. The brochure or menu card that you develop will become your walking advertisement (Figures 3-11, 3-12). Be sure it says who and what you are. Your level of quality and image must be portrayed on that brochure. The question may arise, do you really need a brochure? Absolutely! It's your best advertising tool so print enough to allow you to really use them. Hoarding the few you print is useless.

Tricks to the Menu

1. Keep it simple with simple descriptions of services. If your clients can't understand it and your receptionist can't explain it, it's too complicated.

2. Don't offer so many different a la carte services that the client becomes confused or disgruntled when she thought she came in for a $50 facial only to leave paying $85 after all the add-ons. This can be a great business killer.

3. Be creative and make the menu enticing (Figure 3-13).

4. If you want the client to choose a particular price range, offer one higher and one lower. Most will take the one in the middle.

5. Always have an expiration date on gift certificates, price lists, and series packages. Additionally, somewhere print "prices subject to change without notice."

FIGURE 3-11 *The day spa brochure is a walking advertisement. Is your image displayed on your brochure?*

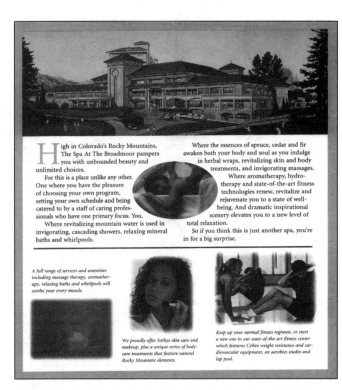

FIGURE 3-12 *A brochure should emphasize the values of the day spa as well as point out the services it offers.*

FIGURE 3-13 *Is your menu fun, like this menu of services by Day Spa Beautique Salon?*

BEAUTY *is a constant state of becoming.* WE *live in a quick fix society. When we sense that something is wrong—with our skin, our bodies, or our lives—we tend to look for an instant solution.* "I'LL *have a facial," we say. "Then I'll feel better."* THE *problem is, one facial won't erase the years of damage that wind, sun, dehydration and stress have done to your skin.* AT *David & Mary, we strive for more than the "feel-good" fix. We are after nothing less than a transformation. In your skin. In your outlook. In the way you feel about taking care of yourself.* WHICH *is why we approach your appointment as a mission, not a timeslot. We will educate you to developments in our field that produce real results. We'll talk about glamour as it relates to your life—not ours. We may want to reenergize your skin by sending it to "boot camp". Or recommend a series of home treatments to fit your budget.* OUR *big-picture approach to beauty is about getting to know you, rather than getting you to buy. If we can't match you with a lipstick you'll actually use, we'll teach you to look wonderful with no lipstick at all.*

FIGURE 3-14 *Let your prospective guests know exactly what you can do for them, as David & Mary, Indianapolis, do in this brochure.*

6. Prioritize the listings in your menu. For example, one hair salon that was converting to a day spa decided to list the skin care and spa services first since her clients were already used to the hair services. She also wanted to develop a big business in package combinations so her packages were listed first.

7. The brochure should contain your mission statement or philosophy of the day spa (Figure 3-14), name and address and even perhaps a diagram of how to get to the salon, hours, and your policies regarding notice of cancellation.

When creating a series or a package, there are basically two ways to make it financially attractive to the client, one being a discount of 5–10 percent on the whole package, making the equivalent of the last treatment free by discounting that amount, or more creatively by including home care products of the value or more you would have discounted anyway. There are advantages to the gift with purchase idea. First of all, it gets the product you want that client to buy in her hands and if it is effective, the repeat purchase is also practically solidified. You can also value it to the client at retail when it only costs you the wholesale price so it's normally less than the value of the free service you would have given. And by having the client use that home care product, the effects of the treatment are further enhanced and client satisfaction is guaranteed. For example, if the regular treatment was $50 and you sold a series of six, the actual total should be

$300. You can either sell the series for $250 or sell it for $300 but give the client a special home care product, such as cream retailing for $60. But your cost on that cream would be only $30, so you save $20 plus the benefits of having the client using the product.

NOTE: *All pricing shown in examples is based on averages and varies greatly from area to area and market to market. Do not necessarily set your pricing on these figures. Revise your pricing according to the market at the time.*

SAMPLE MENUS
Basic Simple Style

Basic deep cleansing facial (deep cleanses skin)	$50.00
Deluxe Treatment (includes exfoliation, ampoule)	$65.00
Enzyme Peel Treatment (AHA-based exfoliation, conditioning)	$65.00
Body Massage	$55.00
Salt Glow Rub (Dead Sea salts, conditioning balm)	$55.00
Full Body Mud Mask (sea mud detox wrap)	$65.00
Full Body Seaweed Treatment (sea algae body smoothing treatment)	$65.00

This menu has advantages and disadvantages. It's clear, concise, and to the point. It's easy to read, not overwhelming, but it doesn't entice and encourage either. It's just a listing. If your clientele is used to your services it's great, but to encourage new business, this format is dull and uninspiring. The following menu expands this format a bit.

Average Menu Style

Basic Deep Cleansing Facial $50.00
(This treatment includes warm steaming, deep pore cleansing, massage, and mask suited to your skin's needs.)

Deluxe Treatment $65.00
(This treatment includes exfoliation of dead cells, luxurious ampoule for nutrition and reconditioning as well as massage and mask suited to your skin's needs.)

(continued on next page)

Body Massage $55.00

(A full hour of relaxing massage, designed to relieve stress and tension according to your body's own condition.)

Salt Glow Rub $55.00

(Special salts from the Dead Sea are mixed with moisturizing and conditioning lotions to slough off dead cells and hydrate while leaving your body feeling smooth and sleek. You'll enjoy the comfortable Vichy shower rinse along with this treatment.)

Full Body Mud Mask $65.00

(After soaking in our hydrotherapy tub, your body will be enveloped in sea mud to soften, smooth, and recondition the skin while you luxuriate in the warm wrap.)

Full Body Seaweed Treatment $65.00

(After your invigorating hydrotherapy treatment, you will be covered with mineral-rich seaweed and wrapped while your body relaxes, reconditions, and rids itself of wastes and toxins.)

Promoting Equipment

Some day spas heavily promote the actual hydrotherapy equipment and some don't. If you have a hydrotherapy tub, it's wise to do so due to the investment made in the tub. The equipment may be included in the description of the service, as in the first example, or as a service by itself.

Hydrotherapy Tub and Underwater Massage $65.00

(Your own private underwater massage and jet exercise treatment; 30 minutes.)

Thalassotherapy/Underwater Massage $65.00
(Hydrotherapy Tub Treatment)

(After receiving your own private underwater massage you'll relax in a combination of seaweed and aromatherapy extracts.)

Dazzling the Reader

Some people like to make the menu sound dazzling. In order to be very detailed about treatment descriptions, a three- or four-fold brochure may be more appropriate to hold all the copy. For example, a treatment may read like this:

Anticellulite Treatment $45.00

This treatment is very effective in helping to prevent or eliminate cellulite. We apply a stimulating aromatherapy formula followed by the seaweed mask. You're wrapped and kept warm to allow increased circulation and metabolism to facilitate the natural removal of cellulite over time. We finish this treatment with the application of an anticellulite contouring cream.

. . . .

SPA POINT

Your brochure and menu make you who you are. Create a great one, print abundantly, and feel free to do mailers. Give them out freely.

. . . .

COMBINATIONS AND PACKAGES

Pricing

It should be kept in mind that there are a myriad of combinations available and people will have their own preferences. The only problem with packages is that clients will always want to make substitutions. To avoid constant substitutions and problems in prices, it may be a good idea to offer a package whereby the client can customize whatever he or she wants. You should determine general price ranges and your limitations on discounts for the package or the value of the gift in accordance with the price of the package. If you're discounting, be sure your discount doesn't exceed 10–15 percent to allow for safety. Don't forget, you may have employees' salaries or commissions. Some people even price the packages according to the time the services will take instead of the normal pricing. For example, if your 1-hour facial is $50, then you might offer a 5-hour package for $250.

Naming and Presenting the Packages

This is a very important part of packaging services. Keep in mind that to many people a day spa is a shortened version of what a spa vacation would be like, so exciting packages and great names for them helps to promote the concept. Packages can be so well done and promoted that they serve to develop the foundation for the whole day spa business. But you must also clearly spell out your requirements and rules. A small day spa can be devastated when a client cancels a full day of beauty. Also, if the day spa is busy, some packages need to be booked a few days ahead to be sure the programming can be set up. Also, be sure makeup and hairstyling are booked last. Most half-day packages run about 3 hours and most full-day packages run 5 hours with 30 minutes to 1 hour for lunch. If you wish to print times in your brochure, be sure you write "approximate time." A package of three services is preferable to only two and too many hydrotherapy-based services is too much. You want to have a good balance in the services you're combining.

> ### THE ULTIMATE GETAWAY FOR A DAY
> TO GET YOU AWAY FOR THE DAY JOIN THE SPIRIT OF THIS ULTIMATE RELAXATION AND REJUVENATION. YOUR DAY WILL INCLUDE A HYDROTHERAPY UNDERWATER MASSAGE, THALASSOTHERAPY RELAXATION TUB TREATMENT, FULL BODY MASK, AND ONE-HOUR SWEDISH MASSAGE, CATERED LUNCH, FACIAL, MANICURE, PEDICURE, AND FINALLY YOUR HAIR AND MAKEUP WILL BE DONE—ALL FOR $350. YOU WILL GO HOME WITH OUR EXQUISITE BODY BATH SET AS OUR SPECIAL GIFT.

> ### THE GENTLEMAN'S EXECUTIVE RETREAT
> DO YOU FEEL STRESSED AND WOULD LIKE TO GET AWAY FOR A QUICK REST AND LOOK GREAT TOO? THIS THREE-HOUR RETREAT PROVIDES YOU WITH A FULL BODY MASSAGE, FACIAL, AND MANICURE. $110 ($130 VALUE)

There are so many ways to name the packages, from themes based on vacations to words related to your day spa name. Be creative and make them very enticing. Now what sort of combinations work well together? The following are some common combinations.

Combinations

- Massage, facial, manicure, pedicure
- Massage, facial, makeup, hairstyle
- Hydrotherapy tub treatment, full body seaweed mask
- Salt glow rub, Vichy shower, full body mud treatment
- Full body mud or seaweed treatment, Vichy shower, massage
- Manicure, pedicure, makeup, hairstyle
- Deep cleansing facial, antistress body massage, spa pedicure
- Hydrotherapy tub, massage, full body mask, manicure, facial
- Aromatherapy body massage, facial, mud body wrap, spa manicure and pedicure, scalp treatment, hairstyle, makeup
- For men: anti-aging facial treatment, muscle relaxing massage, aromatherapy scalp treatment, cleansing manicure and pedicure

Needless to say, the combinations are endless and left only to your imagination and capabilities. As your day spa services evolve, you will quickly learn which services to combine with which for your clientele. In the meantime, it is a good idea to visit other day spas in your area or market niche to learn what they offer. Traveling around and collecting other brochures is very valuable for background ideas.

· ·

SPA POINT

Packages can make the day spa and help the consumer understand that he/she doesn't necessarily have to take a full spa vacation to benefit from the services destination spas offer. Make your packages creative, unique, and enticing.

· ·

Synopsis

Development of the actual spa program must be based on a well-planned concept from the research into the target market, competition, and financial factors on into the choice of treatments. The choice of treatments will often be determined by the hydrotherapy issues—with or without a wet room, with shower, and so forth. Some treatments are more effectively and profitably offered with wet rooms. Then, the development of packages, verbiage on the menu, and presentation of the literature are integral to the success of the entire operation. The finer the planning and literature presentation, often the better the consumer reception. This is a vitally important chapter and well worth a second reading in order not to miss important factors.

Review

1. What does target market mean?
2. Why is a financial analysis important?
3. What are some of the body treatments commonly done in a spa?
4. If you purchase a hydrotherapy tub, why is it important to promote it heavily?
5. What is the advantage of offering packages over individual services?

CHAPTER 4
Purchasing for Your Day Spa

> NOTE: *Please give ample time to your study of this chapter. This is perhaps the heart of the book and an area where so many mistakes are often made. Remember that some of your purchasing decisions are permanent or semi-permanent, so lack of in-depth research on your part could potentially seriously hurt your business.*

OVERVIEW

This is a critical part of the day spa development. If there is ever an area that can be problematical, purchasing is it. A novice to this industry may be exposed to so many options, so much hype, too many promises and choices. The decision-making process can become so confusing that the day spa owner often feels lost. The spa owner may make costly mistakes that cannot easily be retrieved or corrected. It's difficult in a book to address your specific circumstances or needs, but there will be some generalizations that will suit all situations. In addition, this chapter will highlight some of the main areas of concern and make suggestions from a variety of approaches.

. . . .

SPA POINT
Purchasing and developing a spa can be very confusing. The successful day spa owner will approach this in a well-organized businesslike manner.

. . . .

GENERAL PRINCIPLES IN PURCHASING FOR THE DAY SPA

As has been discussed briefly in other chapters, the overall goals you hope to achieve will make a difference in determining your day spa needs. Consider some of the following questions and then answer them on your own. It is recommended that you take a notebook and jot down your answers. Your initial concepts will be beneficial in all areas of spa development but particularly in purchasing.

QUESTIONS FOR CONSIDERATION

1. Why do you want to own a day spa?
2. Do you know your target market? What is your desired client base?
3. If you intend to cater to a broad-based market, list the primary groups (teenagers, men, career middle aged women, etc.) you intend to serve and specifics of each group.

---

4. Do you plan to hire a day spa consultant or do you feel qualified to determine all your own needs?
5. Have you chosen the specific desired size, space, and location?
6. Have you determined the mood, decor, and ambiance for the day spa? Any thoughts on the layout?
7. Have you set a dollar budget for the project?
8. Will you need to obtain financing from outside sources?
9. What are your desired services, products, and timing for opening the day spa?
10. Who is responsible for the business planning and decisions? Who will manage the spa?
11. Is your management person(s) a licensed professional in the industry?
12. How do you intend to hire and train your spa staff?
13. Will your staff be hired as employees or independent contractors?
14. What benefits, if any, do you plan to offer your employees?
15. How quickly do you expect to show a net profit?

"Don't start a new business without having goals, funds, proper training, and plenty of rest up! Don't consider this as a job; the minute you decide it's your career it gets in your system and it's fun. Also, business can't be just money, money, money!"—Lynn Kirkpatrick, With Class, A Day Spa, Tyler, Texas

These questions are but a few you should ask yourself before going into the business. You may want to seek the advice of friends, your suppliers, or others in the industry or hire a professional consultant. But you must consider all these questions before embarking on opening a business. It may even seem that some of the employee questions are irrelevant for this subject, but the reality is that you can't consider pricing your products or services without some idea of your total labor costs. And this may affect your purchasing choices as well. There's a big difference in buying for a small one-person salon or a large day spa employing fifty or more people. So, let's look at a few of these questions for a moment.

· ·

SPA POINT

A good logical assessment of your thoughts will go a long way in developing a solid base for effective purchasing. Making notes of your thoughts well in advance of actually developing the project will help you be more successful.

· ·

Why Do You Want to Own Your Own Day Spa?

If your answer to this is to earn a quick easy buck since the cosmetic industry is so rich then you're in the wrong business. This business takes two or more years to really become profitable. It's very labor and service intensive. If you're looking for quick, easy money, you're better off purchasing a lot of lottery tickets. If, however, you believe in health maintenance, love people, want to help someone improve, enjoy science and technology, believe in beauty, get excited about new trends in products and services then this is the business for you.

Another question you should consider is your own ability to handle the business side of it. Do you have a love for the hands-on but don't care about business, accounting, or money? If so, you either need to reconsider whether you should own your own day spa or be sure you have a trustworthy, qualified partner to help with that side. A wonderful massage won't protect and nurture your business alone. In fact, it's almost more important to be better at business than at treatment if you plan to do both and want the business to be successful. You also need to consider your short-term goals as well as long-term direction. The reasons for opening a day spa may dictate your short- and long-range planning. Is your desire to own a large business or a small personal operation? This will also affect all your other plans.

. . . .

SPA POINT

Probably the most important thing for you to consider before spending money is your reason for wanting a day spa to start with. Are your motives based on solid thinking or just a whim? If it's a whim, you may not make it. Are you willing to lose money for a whim?

. . . .

Do You Know Your Target Market?

As has been discussed in other areas of this book, your target market will determine the criteria for nearly everything. Later in this chapter, we will break the market up into three broad divisions for the sake of simplicity, but you must know to whom you want to cater. This will delineate clearly your monetary and budgetary requirements. You don't want to make the mistake of trying to sell exclusive and expensive products to a lower income market. It won't balance. Hence, your product and equipment purchase must reflect the nature of your potential clientele. If your clientele is upscale, your equipment and product lines should also have an upscale image. Your salon decor and presentation must also follow suit. If your market is to be broad based, you'll still need to identify the major anticipated part of your client mix in order to determine your budget for everything.

. . . .

SPA POINT

As will be stressed throughout this book, knowing your target market will determine all your purchasing, presentation, and overall success potential.

. . . .

HIRING A PROFESSIONAL CONSULTANT

The money you invest in a qualified spa consultant may be the best dollar you ever spend. Unless you are a practicing technician in the business and have a great deal of experience you may need to work with an expert to give you some general guidance. But if you choose to work with a consultant, be sure to check the person out to assure that he/she has the kind of experience or background that will suit your needs. Once your consultant has been chosen, you should develop a meeting agenda with a definite plan for discussion. You must make a list of the many questions and areas of information that you need answered. If you are paying that person per hour or per day, you need to make the most of your time.

By being organized and having an agenda, you will be able to keep the conversation on the topic and moving along. It also tells the consultant that you are serious and plan to keep to business. A good consultant will appreciate your organization and attention to business. If you hire a consultant for a day and then merely sit down and say, "I want a spa, what do I do?" you may waste a lot of your time because that consultant will need to help you get your facts together. All of the questions listed previously will help guide the consultant as well. You particularly need to be prepared to discuss budgets. The more prepared you are in advance of the meeting, the more effective your consultant will be. It may also be that with good organization and a timely meeting, you may not need the consultant more than once.

There are two types of consultants.

Independent Consultant (The Consultant Who Only Consults for a Living)

This person makes money strictly by giving you advice and developing programs. This person will recommend suppliers for products and equipment. At this point, if the consultant is purely an adviser, you should confirm that he/she has no commercial interest in the companies recommended or by referral fees. There's nothing wrong with that, but it's good to know that the recommendations may be somewhat biased. It often means a safe bias though because the recommendation may come as a result of a successful track record of working together. It's just important to know why those specific suppliers are recommended.

Supplier Consultant (The Consultant Who Also Supplies Products and Equipment)

There are many of this type of consultant in the market. This is also fine, but it's important for you to clearly define what advice and services are being offered at no charge because of the potential product or equipment sale and what is reasonable to be charged for. Equipment and product suppliers shouldn't be expected to design and develop your spa just because you're purchasing from them. But at the same time, if the content of the consulting is directly related to the merchandise being sold, it wouldn't be appropriate to pay an additional consulting fee for something that should be part of the sale anyway. This will be further discussed later.

You might suggest that the consultation phase be clear, with the consultant providing any number of suppliers for investigation later. If the client is also interested in the products of the supplier consultant, the consultant must then take off the consultant hat after the consultation and only then begin to present that company's offer. It should be handled professionally by the consultant, but it's up to the client to clearly define the desired limitations of both.

AREAS OF CONSIDERATION

*Space, Location,
Mood, Decor*

This will be discussed later and in chapter 6 in detail, but it's important to keep the location itself in mind when preparing your budget. Obviously the actual spa is a major expense, and it must coincide with your market goals, overall development, and presentation.

*Budget, Financing,
Timing*

This will be covered in detail later in this chapter, but it's also an integral part of spa development. In fact, everything should be based on a budget. The funding issues will clearly determine the scale of the day spa.

*Management
Responsibility, Job
Descriptions*

This will be handled in chapter 7 more fully but suffice it to say at this point that even job descriptions, positions, and the like are cost factors that must be considered and will, therefore, affect your purchasing power. Whether you are the manager or hire one will make a big dent in capital.

PURCHASING CATEGORIES

Before actually discussing the four categories for consideration when purchasing, please refer back to chapter 2 to review the descriptions for the three broad classifications of day spas—luxury market, upper middle market, and middle market. Although the three don't represent all possibilities for spas, it makes it somewhat easier for you to consider for the sake of purchasing and other developmental needs. So for the sake of discussion, most things will fit into one of the following spa types.

1. High luxury market

2. High middle market

3. Middle market

As you begin to develop your spa program, you will be purchasing a lot of things, from supplies and merchandise related to the property itself to the products and equipment. You must realize at the outset that your various suppliers aren't terribly concerned with your budget in areas not affecting them, so there is a natural and expected tendency for a supplier to sell you as much in their area of specialty as possible without regard for the other areas you need to finance as well. You must not forget this. Your job will be to balance between all areas, and if your suppliers really care, to let

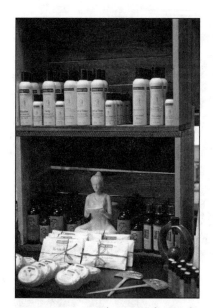

FIGURE 4-1 *Purchasing professional products is an important part of your day spa program development.*

them know that there are limitations in the budget for their segment, if in fact there are limitations. Some day spas are opened with unlimited budgets and that's great, but not terribly realistic. There are four major areas to keep in mind when purchasing:

1. Salon development, decor, the space itself.

2. Professional (in-salon-use products) and retail products. This should include products for face, body, sun care, and makeup. It may also include a budget for boutique items if that is also planned (Figure 4-1). It will also include other necessary supplies and accessory items for use and sale.

3. Professional equipment for the face and body treatments.

4. Survival money for salaries, literature, advertising, promotional pieces. Two to six months' worth of survival savings is recommended.

All four must be kept in mind when setting budgets, but the most immediately vital part of this is your products. Keep in mind that retail is the fastest avenue to generating revenue to put back into the business. Furniture and fixtures are costly but must be amortized out for expensing. So many salons have made the grievous mistake of spending too much money on facial and body equipment only to have no money left in the end to buy the products that turn the cash over the quickest in the business. And then they wonder why they can't make it.

. . . .

SPA POINT

It's imperative to keep a balance of spending in the categories of decor, equipment, products, and survival. They're all important but purchasing and selling retail products turns cash back into the business the fastest. So retail products should have a high priority.

. . . .

CHOOSING PRODUCT AND EQUIPMENT SUPPLIERS

Although a lot of mistakes can be made in designing and purchasing the flooring, wall coverings, and decorations for the day spa, the core of the business will be in the choice of professional equipment and products (Figure 4-2). A person looking in from the outside may feel that the fabrics and mirrors are the most important part, but the reality is that they may draw the client into the spa but won't keep the client coming in. The bottom line for the day spa client now and for the future is simply effectiveness. It may seem to the novice or person looking into the beauty industry from the outside that all products and equipment are the same and that all companies are similar. This is simply not true. For the most part, the professional beauty industry is comprised of well-established companies with integrity, but that's not always the case. Many considerations should be given prior

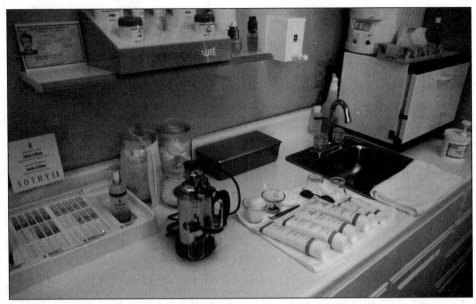

FIGURE 4-2 *Not all products and professional equipment are the same. Discuss your options with other business owners as well as with your product supplier.*

to choosing the products. It is the opinion of this author that choosing your supplier from a business standpoint is more important than choosing a product that appeals to you. The following suggestions may be hard to check out in some cases, but you will want to talk to other salon owners in the business, visit trade shows, talk to experts, and investigate the backgrounds. Consider the following.

Credibility

This is very difficult to determine. You can't just say arbitrarily that if a company has been in business a long time that it's wonderful. On the other hand it is one guideline to help you decide. The esthetics industry is rather small and longevity generally stands for a lot. Well-established companies have the experience to help you with specific problems because they've most likely encountered many of the problems with which you need help. The operations base may be so solid that they have the resources to help you in many unexpected areas. This is not to say that a new company doesn't have credibility. In some cases, newer companies are very service minded and energetic. In either case, find out who the principals of the company are, their background in the business, and their reputation.

· ·

SPA POINT

It goes without saying that you should do business with companies that have a successful track record and good reputation. This is often determined by working with well-established companies but may also be applicable to new companies. Check them out in advance.

· ·

Delivery

It makes absolutely no difference if the products are wonderful if you can't get them or they don't ship for several weeks. Be sure the company has a solid, reasonable shipping record. Find out the normal length of time for order processing from order placement to shipment. A normal reasonable length of time from order to receipt is about five to ten days depending on the distances involved. It is also your responsibility to order your products in a professional manner. Don't wait until you're out of stock to place an order. The time of the day and the day of the week you order also make a difference. It's always better to order early in the day and early in the week. Orders placed late in the day can't get out due to shipping companies' pick-up times. Also, an order placed on Friday might not be shipped until Monday or Tuesday of the next week.

For most companies, the problem is not the shipping time from order to posting, but rather problems of back-ordering (being out of product). This can and does happen to every company from time to time, but excessive back-order situations can be a sign of problems. You will certainly have more time lag on a back-order with imported product lines than locally manufactured products, but the experienced importer is accustomed to this and the problem won't happen often.

. . . .

SPA POINT

Good delivery from your supplier is a must. Watch for a bad history of back-order problems. Additionally, be a responsible client and project your product needs in advance. Order product early in the day and week.

. . . .

Education

This is by far the most important criterion for a supplier. Do they provide education for their products and equipment? How is this education provided? Do you travel to their education center or do they come to you? At first you may think it's better that the supplier come to you, but this isn't always the best scenario. Two problems occur. If the product line is broad, it's unrealistic to expect that the supplier can bring all the products to you for training. Additionally, it's very easy for you and your staff to get distracted and called away to handle things when the training is done in your business. This is very bad for both you and the supplier. The opportunity for you and your staff to attend training in the supplier's training center or even at a designated hotel provides more concentration on your part and the ability for you to get away. It also offers you an opportunity to meet with other professionals in your area. Often your best friends for life come out of meetings in product classes.

It's also beneficial to have your supplier do some classes on your premises, particularly if you have several staff members trained at once. Many of the product suppliers in this industry also offer other classes on a variety of subjects beside products. This is advantageous to you because on breaks you may also learn more about how specific techniques will fit into your

"It's so difficult training, retraining, training, and retraining your people."—Ginny Burge, Day Spa Beautique Salon, Houston, Texas

product usage. It is important, however, that if the classes are promoted as generic technical training they don't inundate you with product information, which reduces the quality of the education to mere product knowledge. That is also fine but should be kept separate, and you should be given a clear distinction between the two.

Ongoing product and service education is the unquestionable mainstay of this business. Your supplier must be there for you in terms of product knowledge education on a regular basis. Most quality esthetic product lines are far too complicated for a one-time quicky education. It has been documented that training on a product line a minimum of once or twice a year dramatically increases sales. It is also a plus if the product line you're choosing has a good complement of educational support materials—manuals, ongoing newsletter or magazine, product videos. This will provide continuing educational support for new staff members as they wait for the next available training opportunity.

· ·

SPA POINT

It is a proven fact that your sales revenue on retail and service is directly related to the quality and frequency of product knowledge training. Your supplier should offer ongoing education to keep you and your staff polished.

· ·

Service

Service is closely related to education in importance. You must work with suppliers who value service. Do you find them pleasant to deal with, or when you call to place a small order do they treat you badly? When you have a problem, will they return your calls and help you? Do they offer suggestions on ways you can increase and improve your business? The service behind the product is what will make you stand out in your spa and the same holds true with suppliers. There are many similarities between companies but the bottom line is, will they be there for you when you need them? Some companies are interested only while you are placing your large initial order. The reality is that you are important to that supplier every day. The reorders are much more important than a big initial order, and a small client has the potential to grow into a big client.

Now you also have a responsibility to your supplier if you want it to be there for you. This will be discussed more fully under choosing product lines, but it's useful at this juncture to mention that you cannot pick a supplier's brain all the time and spend only $50 a month. The more you purchase within your size and category potential, the more that supplier can afford to take care of you. The same will be true for you with your own clients. You will help and support the client who can't spend much money but is devoted to you and your products more than the fickle client who demands a tremendous amount of your time but hops around between salons, department stores, and every hot new item advertised in a magazine or on television.

. . . .

SPA POINT

A good quality client and supplier require the same effort. It's a matter of devotion and support, not just dollar volume. It all comes down to quality service and mutual support. A pleasant, caring, supportive supplier can make a huge difference in the quality and success of your business.

. . . .

DISTRIBUTION CHANNELS

In general, purchasing products and equipment is a bit different in the professional esthetic and day spa market than in the mainstream cosmetology field.

Beauty Supply House

Historically, product distribution in the hair and nail market has been done predominantly by the major beauty supply house chains located all over America. Many fine hair care companies also market their esthetic lines this way. A few exclusive esthetic lines may also market through this avenue. If you come from a cosmetologist background and are going into esthetics and day spas, your instinct will be to look to this method of distribution. Within this channel, most of the education is also supplied by national educational teams that do classes at beauty supply house shows. The sales representatives working for these supply houses are usually trained in the products to some extent, but their primary job is to visit with you on a local basis and help you with your ordering while counting on the national educational teams to do the product knowledge training. Based upon the rep or by your phone call, most supply houses provide a delivery service for the products ordered in areas where a supply house is located. This is not, however, the normal channel of distribution for esthetics.

Esthetic Distribution

There is still a difference in the size of the traditional hair and nail market. There are many more hairdressers than estheticians and massage therapists. As a result, esthetics doesn't have the marketing base yet to warrant the previous method of distribution. Additionally, most full face, body, and makeup lines are somewhat complicated and as such not suited to the more mass method of distribution and education. To date, the majority of skin care lines are distributed directly by the manufacturer/importer or by special esthetic distributors (Figure 4-3). The manufacturer or distributor may also have sales representatives to assist in the sales and service of products.

It's common for the potential buyer to think it's advisable to bypass the distributor or representative in favor of purchasing directly from the manufacturer. The thinking behind this is to save money and cut out the middle person. In most cases the buyer doesn't save money and also loses a person who can help on a much closer basis. The commissions for representatives and distributors are covered by the manufacturer or the distributor if the representative is working for the distributor. The difference in distribution from the manufacturer, distributor, and representative follows.

FIGURE 4-3 *Professional skin products will comprise a large portion of your supplies.*

MANUFACTURER

In this case all training and product knowledge is handled from the head office, wherever that may be. In the industry we use the term *manufacturer* to describe the person or company that makes the product, has it made by a laboratory, or imports it from foreign countries. The client deals exclusively with the staff of the manufacturer/importer. This has the advantage of speed and clarity of information. The disadvantage is that the manufacturer may be responsible for the entire nation and therefore not have enough time to concentrate on individual customers.

DISTRIBUTOR

A distributor is a complete company in its own right and operates under an exclusive distribution contract with the manufacturer, normally for a specified territory. The distributor actually purchases the products from the manufacturer and stocks them for local or regional distribution. The training and service is handled exclusively by the distributor except in cases where the manufacturer is also involved in a project.

REPRESENTATIVE

A representative may work for the manufacturer or distributor. Both manufacturers and distributors use the services of reps to improve the sales and service of the product distribution. In some cases the rep is a salesperson and in some case a licensed technical trainer or both. The role of the rep is normally to be out in the field helping existing clients while building new ones in a specific local area. Again, the commission normally paid to the rep comes from the margin of the manufacturer or distributor.

The existence of this position will almost never affect the salon price for goods. And in most cases distributors and reps are your best level of personal support. Take advantage of their desire and ability to help you. It is perhaps useful to let your distributor or manufacturer know if you feel your rep isn't servicing you well, is trying to oversell you, or is generally ignoring you. As large as all territories are, it's difficult for the company to know everything going on out in the field and your input will help keep the company well polished.

· ·

SPA POINT

Whether you purchase directly from the manufacturer or through your local distributor or rep, the important thing to remember is that the esthetic industry is different. You will most often receive your products by mail over a period of a week to ten days. Your local rep or distributor is really your friend and helper in expanding your business, answering questions, and educating you and your staff.

· ·

CHOOSING PRODUCT LINES

The question I'm probably asked the most is, "What product line should I go with?" or "How do I choose a product?"

The four business criteria mentioned previously (credibility, delivery, education, service) should be foremost in your mind as you investigate product lines. Beyond that, there are a number of considerations depending on your market, budget, and goal.

Products Are Not Created Equal

Many people would like to say that all product lines are basically the same. This author doesn't agree. There are certainly similarities among product lines, but there are vast degrees of quality and variation. You might want to consider skin care lines in a similar manner as wine. If you go into a shop selling wines, you'll probably find hundreds of different reds, whites, and rosés all packaged in bottles, jugs, or boxes. Are all the wines the same? The common denominator is that all the wines are wine and assumably drinkable. There are wines for $3, $30, $300, or even $3,000.

In the cosmetic industry people like to say all the money, and difference between products, is in the packaging. Would that hold for wine? I don't think so. Even though packaging can be a very expensive aspect of cosmetics, it's still minimal if the product line concerned has very large distribution. As expensive as it may be, the marketing advantage will more than cover any additional packaging cost. The reality is that there's as much quality variance in cosmetics as in wines. The packaging is only one issue. Other determinants include the blend of ingredients, the derivation and quality of the raw materials, the actual manufacturing process, and the distribution. These are all as important to cosmetics as the soil, temperature, and rainfall are to wine.

I'll Test It on Myself

Many people make their choice of product lines based on testing a few products on their own skin. Although it's desirable and wonderful if the products are suitable and improve your skin, self-testing is far from suffi-cient. To say that all clothes in a boutique sell only to people with my taste would obviously be limiting to the potential buyers. The same is true for foods. Some people are so allergic to seaweed that it's life threatening, but to others it's fine. The point here is that it's great to test products on your-self, but if you plan to use human testing as your criterion for choosing a product line, you must test the entire line on numerous people—not just a couple of products and not just a few people.

Free Products

Will the product company give you products for this test? Most likely they cannot and will not. The reality is that this is an industry of relatively small manufacturers compared with the Estee Lauders and Revlons of the world. If they gave products away to everyone who showed interest in the line, the company would go broke. If the company offers samples or trial sizes, whether for free or for sample purchase, it's really the responsibility of the buyer to purchase the products. Sometimes a company will offer you a few products. Be grateful and pleased but don't expect it. If you demanded free products from potential suppliers and they were unable to supply them you might have an unjustifiable negative impression of the product lines. In the end you might lose out on a good line. Additionally, if a company overtly offers you many free products to test, remember the value of something free. Be logical. Would you give your potential clients free full-size products?

American Made Versus European or Other Imported Lines

What a controversial question this becomes. To the company marketing an imported line, European or imported is always better. Well-established Eu-ropean lines certainly have a long history and solid background. To the American producer, the reply is that American lines are more alive, more high-tech, and more up-to-date. Which view is correct? They're both cor-rect. There are certainly pluses with European lines in that the Europeans have a much longer history of good skin care and product development. In most cases, products that are developed are well tested before reaching this country, which gives another level of confidence and safety. Some even break down the imports further through preferences among French, Ger-man, Spanish, Oriental, and other countries. These variations may be im-portant to you and your market as a matter of choice.

On the other hand, American ingenuity is also available in cosmetic science. American manufacturer's research and development is fast, inno-vative, and efficient. Many of the greatest cosmetics on the market the world over owe their beginnings to American research. The products hit the mar-ket more quickly and address trends more readily. The down side to this may be a too-rushed approach that can also backfire down the road. The choice between the two is again a matter of preference but be sure the business criteria support your choice.

Branded Versus Private Label

Branded lines are those that are marketed through salons and day spas with a specified name, a brand as developed by a manufacturer. Private label means a product that is packaged in a generic container that you may name and label with whatever you want. The basic formula may exist for any number of clients with each one naming it something else. There are advantages and disadvantages to both. The branded lines often carry with them national or international name value due to advertising and marketing. Additionally, as a general rule, branded lines also have a lot of support materials such as packaging, samples, bags, posters, brochures, and other literature.

Private label means just that. You may save money on the product itself and have a much larger markup to work with, but you, in essence, become the manufacturer. It will be up to you to develop your own support systems, including packaging, bags, samples, and literature. If that, for whatever your marketing goals are, isn't necessary, then the high profit margins make private label for you very attractive. However, if you have an upscale day spa with an image you need to portray in your product, by the time you spend the money to develop all the support, you will find your margins greatly reduced, sometimes to below the margin you would have if you had chosen a branded line. On the other hand, if you have a day spa and have developed a very strong name in your area, you may be ready to put your name on a line because the value of your name will make it a strong sell. If you are augmenting a branded line with items to fill in the holes you find, you may do well with private label. There's a place for both.

Support Materials

Although the subject of support materials was touched on previously, this should be another important consideration in your choice of lines. If you plan to do a lot of mailings or group lectures, or want educational materials in the day spa, you will find this an important contribution to your decision. It's nearly impossible for you to produce your own samples due to the volume required by most manufacturers. Most often the minimum requirement to produce a sample is 25,000 of each or more. If you cannot use a large amount of samples in a short period of time, you risk the sample going bad, and this could kill your business. Therefore, if the samples are important be sure to look for a line that offers them.

Quality literature is also expensive. It's helpful if your product line offers client-oriented brochures along with bags, posters, training videos, manuals, and information. These may seem secondary to the line itself, but they are quite important.

Retail Price Structure/ Professional Treatments

The line you choose should offer some specialized professional treatments that cannot be done at home to keep the client returning to the salon (Figure 4-4). In addition, the actual retail line should be packaged and priced overall to suit your target market. Most lines on the market now offer 100 percent markup. That means that if you buy it for $5 you will sell it for $10. Currently most lines available on the market are geared to the middle class income and up. Your target market will help you determine if the line is priced too high or too low.

Although a manufacturer cannot legally fix the price of the products for retail, they will offer a suggested retail. It is customary in this industry to

Erica's, a prestigious but quietly exclusive Day Spa offers a careful selection of face, body, and cosmetic treatments for the discerning client. Internationally known Estheticians and CIDESCO Diplomates, Erica Miller and Paula Dean, with combined expertise of over 30 years, have developed the finest in treatments and products from around the world to serve all your esthetic needs. Our staff is highly trained and stays on top of the industry's latest technology and scientific developments to better serve you. With SOTHYS Paris, a complete range of over 125 products and treatments, we have extraordinary capability to treat all your skin's needs on a customized personal basis. Don't wait another day to discover the best and most vibrant You that you can be. Call 352-9406 for your appointment today.

FACIAL CARE TREATMENTS:

Deep Cleansing European Facial Treatment:
Treatment begins with in-depth analysis of the skin, followed by deep pore cleansing or surface active peeling, European and/or Oriental massage, and customized skin correction treatment through specialized ampoules, serums, and masks specially selected according to your skin's needs.
(Approximate time: 1 hour) $55.00

Deluxe French Institute Treatments:
Highly unique and specialized, these high-tech treatments are chosen after an in-depth cleansing and analysis for your skin's specific needs for superior results on dehydrated, aging, flaccid, and oily/acne skins. These treatments may also be recommended on a series basis and when taken as a course of 6 weekly treatments, you will receive a specialized home care treatment product valued at between $50.00 and $75.00. Treatments offered include the SOTHYS Paris Oxydermie, Collagen & Hyaluronic

Acid, Deep Lifting, Biocollaspheres, and Sebum Regulating Treatments. Treatments may be combined and varied according to your skin's specific needs. In addition, in these extended treatments, you will also receive specialized care for your hands and feet.
(Approximate time: 1 - 1 1/2 hours)

Treatment: $65.00 - $75.00
Series of 6: $385.00 - $450.00

Warm paraffin masks or the very cool Kooli mask may be added to most treatments to enhance product absorption for an additional $10.00.

BODY SPA TREATMENTS:

Our variety of body spa treatments has been carefully selected and developed to facilitate the improvement of your skin, reduction of stress and fatigue and general development of well being. We incorporate the use of aromatherapy, plant, and biological extracts. Whether your interest is traditional Swedish massage or more concentrated care, our professionals will customize a program to suit your personal needs. For all custom spa packages you will receive an additional 15% discount on the total of the services received where two or more services are combined. Normally, three treatments combined may be done in 1 1/2 to 2 hours which will save you time and enhance the results of any individual treatment. Each Body Spa Service is approximately 1 hour long.

Swedish Body Massage	$50.00
Aromatherapy Body Massage	$55.00
Shiatsu Body Massage	$60.00
Salt Glow with Body Conditioning	$50.00
Anti-Cellulite or Anti-Stress Spot Trmt.	$50.00
Conditioning Sea Mud Body Mask	$65.00
Sea Algae Body Spa Treatment	$65.00
Deluxe French Bust Treatment/Mask	$65.00
Deep Cleansing Back Treatment	$55.00

WAXING:

We use the world famous CIREPIL family of French Depilatory waxes. Superfluous hair removal provides a longer lasting and more effective method of hair removal than shaving, bleaching, or using depilatory creams.

Face:	forehead/hairline	$15.00 - $20.00
	brows/lips/chin	$10.00 - $15.00
	full face	$25.00 - $45.00
Body:	neckline	$10.00 - $20.00
	underarms	$15.00 - $25.00
	back/shoulders	$30.00 - $45.00
	hands/feet	$10.00 - $25.00
	1/2 arms/legs	$15.00 - $35.00
	full arms/legs	$25.00 - $65.00
	bikini	$25.00 - $40.00
	full body	$150.00 - $250.00
Lash & Brow Tints:		$10.00 - $15.00

NAIL CARE SERVICES:

All of our nail care services are based upon caring for healthy well groomed nails. We use the finest in products and observe rigid sanitary practices in all treatments. Our spa treatments include exfoliation, special algae or mud conditioning and aromatherapy massage.

Basic Manicure/Pedicure	$15.00 - $25.00
Spa Manicure/Pedicure	$30.00 - $50.00
Addition of Paraffin	$5.00 - $10.00
Polish Change	$10.00 - $15.00

FIGURE 4-4 *Does your spa menu offer specialized professional treatments, like this menu for Erica's, A Day Spa, in Dallas?*

closely follow the suggested retail price. Some like to add a dollar or two to cover possible freight costs. But it is dangerous to sell your products too high or too low on a nationally distributed line. Your clients will have problems and your credibility may come into question. If you want to totally specify your own pricing, you may want to consider the private label route.

It is logical to assume that if you're selling to a very wealthy upscale client high-priced products will sell well. If, however, you are attempting to sell expensive products to a lower class market, you will probably have some resistance. This is a basic pricing concept, but since the day spa is generally considered to be an upper middle class and above entity, most lines available on the market today should not receive much price resistance. Remember that if your clients care enough about their skin to visit your day spa, they also have the wherewithal to spend money on their skin if that is truly a priority. I always like to remind estheticians and massage therapists that clients come in for a reason. That person's face or body is the only one she's ever going to get. The cost is minimal, particularly if you break down the retail cost to a per-day usage. Practically speaking, no lines are too expensive if the priority is evident and the educational process takes place properly.

Purchasing Multiple Lines

If you know what you're doing and why you want more than one product line, there's no problem. However, the more lines you have the more complicated your business becomes. In the beginning, it is normally wise to choose one very complete line and then add other lines for specific reasons later. If the line is diverse and broad enough, it should cover most of your needs. There is a learning curve involved in effectively using a product line and this time can be confused by having multiple lines. In addition, if problems or reactions occur, determining the problem becomes more complicated. Additionally, when more than one line is used, it becomes difficult if not impossible to hold the manufacturer responsible for any problems that might occur.

As a simple financial matter the more you invest with one supplier the more that company can afford to support you in return. There are so many day spas with three to five lines, bits and pieces of so many things, the question arises as to the reason. The result is a confused customer and small inventories of many lines with no real product line support. In some cases you're also indirectly telling your clients it's okay to mix in other lines that you're not selling. How can you expect your client to be loyal to a product line if you're not? Granted, there may be a difference because you are the licensed professional, but it's hard for the client to see that.

And finally, unless there's a specific reason for a variety of lines and products, you could be surprised by how much extra money you may have tied up in products, money that could be used elsewhere. There are, however, some situations in which you would want multiple lines. A typical situation would be where you have an expensive upscale line and a modest inexpensive line for your teenagers, beginners, and lower market clients. You may even offer this lesser line on purpose to get a client started and then graduate that person up as the educational process proceeds. This is a common marketing tactic that works well. You may also keep one broad complete line as your overall main line and offer some specialty niche lines for specific issues. An example might be a line for comedogenic skins or for camouflage makeup.

Ingredient Trends, Fads, and Myths

Just as in the fields of fashion, automobiles, and restaurants, there are fashionable issues related to cosmetics. The trends are very obvious in the campaigns surrounding color cosmetics. Most major lines come out with changes and trends in colors a couple of times a year. Color trends in makeup are known also by the consumer so it's important that your makeup line provide periodic additions and stories to help you market the line and stay up to date. The lesser-known fact is that there are also trends and fads in skin and body care. These trends are more often presented as negatives rather than new substances. In order to differentiate a line, a manufacturer may choose to use ingredients and treatment concepts to negate others, or a new hot ingredient may make one line appear to stand out.

Rebecca James Gadberry, probably the nation's greatest expert in the field of cosmetic chemistry and ingredients, states, "There are no bad ingredients in cosmetics. There are appropriate and non-appropriate uses for all ingredients." You cannot judge a line only by looking at an ingredient label, at whether it contains mineral oil, animal extracts, aloe vera, or AHAs (alpha hydroxy acids). It's not that simple, and none of these ingredients are necessarily good or bad, depending on the usage. Nor can you judge a line by simple terms like "all natural," "hypoallergenic," "organic," or "fragrance free." These are loose terms that are easily misinterpreted without more knowledge. As an example, "fragrance free" merely means that the product contains no synthetic perfumes, but it's a known fact that even pure, natural essential oils can also cause reactions. "Hypoallergenic" means that the product has been tested by some to be less allergy prone; it doesn't mean that it's reaction proof. It's important and valuable to study ingredients, and you should obtain a copy of *Milady's Skin Care and Cosmetic Ingredients Dictionary* by Natalia Michalun with M. Varinia Michalun.

Above and beyond this you should learn more about the manufacturing process of a cosmetic. The order of mix, or the way in which the product is mixed together, is often more critical to a product than what's actually in it. The derivation of the raw materials and how they are prepared make a difference. You can no more make a pie with only a list of ingredients than you can maintain your health by taking a vitamin C capsule alone. A well-thought-out, sophisticated, high-quality line is a result of tremendous research, energy, money, and testing. If that product contains a specific substance that may be on today's no-no list, then you should investigate the reasoning before categorically eliminating the product. There's probably a very logical and important reason why the ingredient is being used.

Skin Care Versus Makeup

You will soon learn when hiring staff that the estheticians and makeup artists out there may be licensed to do both but as a rule gravitate to one or the other. We will not discuss personality types here, but it's important to keep that in mind when purchasing. You'll either need to be sure to have staff for both areas or stock heavier in makeup or skin. In branded lines, makeup can be a costly part of the initial investment.

Makeup is a necessity, but it will normally not claim client loyalty to the degree skin care will. Women will just as easily float through a department store and purchase the latest colors or buy based on the gift-with-purchase item available. If you have a display for the makeup you need to be sure to stock all that is visible. You will never know when that color you didn't carry is desirable. If your line has fifteen lip or eye pencils you'll normally need them all. Makeup is an impulse buy based a great deal on the visual aspect and most clients feel more availability is better.

If you're planning to have a strong makeup department, then you'll need to stock more heavily and completely. Be prepared for more stock to sit on the shelves than in skin care. As a result, it may be frustrating, but on the other hand, makeup is self-explanatory and your client knows what to do with a lipstick. So the products will sell themselves more than skin care products. If you are purchasing branded skin care and have a limited budget, you may want to consider private label for your makeup. You have the ability to purchase a lot more for less money. Or you may purchase some branded and some private label.

THE ACTUAL PURCHASE

It's nearly impossible to suggest how much you should spend on skin care products and makeup. (By the way, in all references to skin care, body and sun care are included as well.) The following suggestions are extremely broad and can be inaccurate depending on the lines you choose. You must really get a suggested budget from the lines you think you are interested in. The pricing is based on branded lines, not private label, and also is broken down into professional and retail, professional being the larger bulk products that are not retailed. For private label, your pricing may be half, one-third, or less. Just keep packaging and image in mind. Private label is not recommended for the high luxury market unless you specifically develop special packaging and literature. Private label makeup may be preferred in the middle market to save on initial investment.

The following figures are based on one to two treatment rooms, so if you plan to stock each treatment room, double your professional figures for each 1-1/2 rooms, the reason being that body rooms will not need the same depth of stock. Also, in many cases body products come in much larger bulk sizes. In very simplistic terms, it might be easy to say that the overall product investment for the three categories might be in the neighborhood of $20,000, $10,000, and $5,000 respectively. Please consult with your suppliers for their general costs and ask about their different investment levels. Also, discuss volume discounts with your suppliers. They may offer free freight for purchases over a certain amount or extra bonuses if you purchase so many. Most suppliers have various promotional programs available to you. Training may also be free with purchases over a certain amount.

NOTE: *Pricing information included here is for study purposes only and may not reflect pricing or market levels at the time of your interest. It has been based on price structures between the years 1994 and 1996. Please adjust for your own current market trends.*

MARKET		PROFESSIONAL	RETAIL
High Luxury,	Skin	$2,000–$5,000	$5,000–$10,000
	Makeup	$ 500–$2,000	$3,000–$10,000
High Middle,	Skin	$1,000–$2,000	$3,000–$ 6,000
	Makeup	$ 500–$1,000	$2,000–$ 5,000
Middle,	Skin	$ 500–$1,000	$1,500–$ 3,000
	Makeup	$ 500–$1,000	$1,000–$ 3,000

SPA POINT

It should be obvious that there are many considerations in choosing a line beyond the issues of credibility, delivery, education, and service. A possible starting point would be to choose a broad-based, branded line for your main line for all the support reasons and then add niche or private label to augment your main product story. You must look at the entire story of the product line, not just an ingredient, the package, the price, or the fragrance. The choices are many but it all boils down to choosing wisely from a good logical business standpoint for your needs.

. . . .

PURCHASING DAY SPA EQUIPMENT

Have you ever bought a car? Well, purchasing equipment for your day spa can be similar. There are some basic differences in quality of various equipment lines, and then there are the differences in the "bells and whistles." This is not to imply that you should just purchase the cheapest line of equipment that's on the market or go to the opposite extreme to purchase the most expensive luxury version either. Your choice, both in price and quality, will be based on your target market and budget.

It is also good to know when you begin pricing lines that you have choices. Because the day spa concept is growing rapidly, supply and demand will soon accelerate price reductions on certain pieces of equipment. Also, with time, equipment pricing goes up and down along with the general market.

Above all, remember that equipment is an amortized cost and your investment will take time to pay off. Equipment manufacturers view a sale as a once in every five to ten years purchase, except for the replacement parts, so their goal will naturally be to sell you as much as possible. If you go in knowing that, you will have more objectivity when finally choosing the items you think you really need. Some general considerations when purchasing follow.

Construction, Durability, Warranties

Just as in buying a car, you may not choose the most luxurious model, but you want equipment that is built well for your needs. Beauty schools often make the mistake of purchasing the cheapest equipment for the school and then have years of nightmares because heavy student usage ruins the equipment too soon. If, on the other hand, you don't anticipate heavy usage and you plan from the beginning to upgrade the equipment in a year or two, then you might be fine with lesser quality.

Most day spa and salon equipment is shipped to you directly from the central manufacturer. When repairs are necessary, smaller, portable equipment must normally be shipped back to the supplier. The warranties and policies in case of repair should be clearly delineated in advance. Most warranties cover parts and labor and are in effect for one to two years. A few companies offer loaner equipment on the smaller items. Turnaround time, that is the length of time it takes to receive, repair, and return the equipment, is an essential question to ask. It's also wise to ask what happens with repairs once the equipment is off the warranty.

It is normally unrealistic to hope that your manufacturer has the equipment available in your area. Most equipment is shipped. Sometimes an advantage of working with a full service distributor that sells both products and equipment is in the service offered when equipment breaks down. The distributor may have the capability of repairing the equipment or loaning you a replacement while yours is being repaired.

Parts/Accessory Items

In almost all cases, the glass electrodes, ventouses, and hoses are expensive to replace. It's imperative that you and your staff take very good care of your equipment. Your policy regarding cleaning, care of, and replacement of broken items should be covered in your employee manual. If you are in a school situation, it is suggested that the glass ventouses and electrodes be sold to the student in the student kit. This will ensure more responsibility on the part of the student and teacher alike. Whether in a school or a day spa, you should keep some extra parts on hand.

Training

Just as with products, you should expect to receive training from the supplier you purchase your equipment from, but there is often confusion as to what level of training is expected and whether it should be free of charge. This is controversial and it's up to you and your supplier to negotiate. Most people purchasing equipment, whether it's facial equipment or spa body equipment, don't have the proper basic training. Therefore, training in how to operate this specific manufacturer's version of the device is normally insufficient. However, should it be the responsibility of that company to teach you how to give a treatment? A close analogy would be if you purchase a car, that dealer will certainly familiarize you with their model, but you would never expect the car dealer to teach you how to drive. So in some viewpoints, equipment sellers are required only to familiarize you with their specific equipment.

On the other hand, the reality in the day spa industry is that most buyers don't know how to operate a hydrotherapy tub or Vichy shower. Therefore, technique training is almost always required. It should be acceptable for the supplier, then, to charge you an additional fee due to the extra time needed to teach you how to give treatments, just as if you enrolled in a driver education class. Some equipment suppliers will happily throw in the training for a large enough purchase. The amount of time for training and fees is an issue that you must discuss and negotiate with your supplier. When purchasing the hydrotherapy equipment, you must further determine where the training will take place, at the supplier's training center or on site in your day spa. If it is done on site, it's quite reasonable for the supplier to charge travel expenses as well. All the training, travel, and incidental expenses should be considered by you when determining your actual equipment costs.

Support and Service

There is no difference here between product or equipment purchasing; the support and caring of your supplier is tantamount to success. You want to choose a supplier that has an ongoing interest in you, not just in a one-time sale. If you're buying your products from a distributor that also handles equipment, you both have a mutual advantage. It behooves that supplier to take good care of you on the equipment because he/she has an ongoing business relationship with you on products. It also improves your position with that supplier and is possibly safer from an overall balance standpoint. That distributor will also have a better idea of your budget as well because of the purchase balance between the products and equipment, hence will be less likely to sell you more than you need. This is not to say that equipment companies are out to get you and sell you too much. They are interested in serving your needs but don't have the concern of your product and survival budget to consider.

FACIAL EQUIPMENT

The subject of facial equipment is covered in *Milady's Standard Textbook for Professional Estheticians* by Joel Gerson and also *Milady's Skin Care Reference Guide* by Dr. Mark Lees, so we won't spend much time on it here. When opening a day spa, you will certainly have facial rooms to equip. It's wise when equipping several rooms to buy the type of equipment that can fit on a stand and be added to.

Naturally the ideal situation is to fully equip each room with a full complement of facial devices and a comfortable facial bed or chair (Figure 4-5). Or, if you are on a tight budget, you may choose to have one skin care machine per two rooms. The pieces may even vary somewhat for the different rooms so that you have some mobile options and more flexibility. You may have a luxurious facial chair in one room but equip another room with a portable massage table that sits up like a chair. Then the room could be used for massage, waxing, or facials as needed. If finances are tight, you may choose

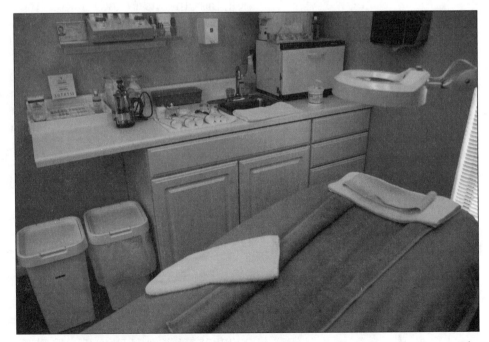

FIGURE 4-5 *All products for skin treatments should be easily accessible in the treatment room. The facial bed and equipment should be prepared before the client enters the room.*

to put a good steamer in your main facial room and then put a hot towel cabinet in another room. Hot towel cabinets are wonderfully useful in all areas of the day spa. They are less expensive than steamers but the versatility allows for growth.

It is the opinion of this author that equipment can be added and upgraded as you grow. But it is not recommended that you use homemade or home-use items such as crock pots or roasters unless they are completely hidden from the client's sight. Although a crock pot can be used to hold hot towels, temperature control can be difficult, they don't hold enough, and, beyond that, the image they create is cheap and unprofessional. This may not be a problem if you are catering to the market that doesn't expect more, but if you are serving a professional career and above upscale market, it will injure the credibility of your business and you may never even be aware of it. It is imperative that whatever you do in the area of equipment be professional and maintain your image.

NOTE: *A word about pricing. This is entirely subjective and may change with time and market needs. Also the author's view of the three market divisions is based upon discussions in chapter 2 and are segmented purely for theoretical purposes. Also, pricing adjustments must be made in deference to the publication date of this book.*

The following price estimates represent a fully equipped facial room, not counting smaller accessory equipment or supplies. This would include a facial chair/bed, magnifying lamp, steamer, full machine with brush, vac/spray, high frequency, galvanic.

High luxury market:	$ 5,000–$10,000
High middle market:	$ 4,500–$ 7,000
Middle market:	$ 2,000–$ 5,000

Accessory equipment needed in a facial room would include paraffin heaters, depilatory wax heaters, wood lamps for analysis, electric masks/mittens/booties/blankets, and the like. These are not particularly high dollar costs but should be considered in the accessory budgets.

BASIC BODY TREATMENT EQUIPMENT

This is a pretty simple category. You will need massage tables in all rooms where massage, body, and/or waxing treatments are being done. A large variety of massage tables are on the market today, everything from electric tables that raise and lower simply by stepping on a foot switch to lightweight portable fold-up tables. There are also wet tables with drainage systems designed for the dry room that can't floor drain. The most important feature when choosing tables is your room (wet or dry) and the durability desired. It's nice to have some portable tables for the flexibility of movement, but it's also good to have very solid, stable tables, particularly in the wet rooms. In a wet room, the tables must be specifically designed to be waterproof. If a stainless steel or plastic table is being used in the wet room, be sure waterproof pads are used and that the feet of the table have rubber or other non-skid feet to provide proper protection on the tile floors. The other massage tables must be comfortable and adjustable for different technician's heights.

High luxury market:	$1,000–$5,000
High middle market:	$ 850–$2,000
Middle market:	$ 600–$1,000

Accessory equipment might include electric bed warmer pads and hydroculators for linen herbal wraps.

HYDROTHERAPY EQUIPMENT

This is the most complicated category to discuss. There are many different equipment modalities and the choice of what to include in your day spa program may be determined by space constraints, budget, client demand, target market, or personal choice. Some day spas begin with nothing more than a shower, and others feel the need to have every possible modality. It is a subjective choice in many cases. The trick to making it work has a lot to do with the treatment planning.

The most expensive piece of equipment is usually the hydrotherapy tub. For some day spas, the cost doesn't equal its marketability. For others, however, the advertising and promotional value of it far outweigh the cost. To force a choice in purchasing equipment for a day spa would be similar to forcing an answer to which is better, steak or lobster? Steak would obviously be better to a meat and potatoes person or one who is allergic to lobster. But to the person who may have grown up on the coast of Massachusetts, the answer might be the reverse. Who's to say? The final choice is yours. But understanding issues related to equipment in general and some of the various equipment options might help with your decision. Most equipment has been described briefly in chapter 2.

Hydrotherapy Issues— Laundry/Hygiene/ Sanitation

Because hydrotherapy is wet, two main issues must be carefully considered—towel usage and hygiene. You will use anywhere from two to ten towels per treatment depending on the treatments. Clean, fresh towels must be used at every juncture. Your laundry will double or triple with the addition of body treatments and hydrotherapy. The more hydrotherapy equipment that is utilized in a given treatment, the more laundry that is produced. You must have an appropriate amount of towel and sheet stock as well as sufficient washers and dryers if you do your own. And who is responsible for taking care of this laundry? You may want to hold your body technicians responsible, as is often the case, but if your day spa is busy, you should consider a helper because your professional technicians' time is better spent in treatment than in the laundry room.

In the same vein, when hydrotherapy is added, the need for absolute impeccable sanitary procedures also increases. Everyone gets excited at the thought of building a 12' × 12' fully tiled wet room for a hydrotherapy tub, but when it comes time to clean, sanitize, and dry both the tub and the room between clients, the issue suddenly changes. The tub and room must be cleaned, disinfected, and dried after each and every client. This can be a major issue in the day spa. It takes about 15 minutes to clean a tub and wet room properly. Who does it? Another issue here is the apparel worn by the technician. They usually get wet and, therefore, need time to change uniform. This is valuable treatment and selling time. Additionally, if the tub purchased doesn't have a power drain, it can take 30 minutes to drain, clean, and drain a tub again. You also need to be certain your tub products are safe to go down the drain.

Whether or not it seems like a big issue to you, the fastest way to kill a hydrotherapy-based business is to fail to clean, sanitize, and dry the area. This is a major consideration when developing the day spa and determining the number of wet rooms and what equipment to offer. Another brief word about sanitation, you must be aware of your local, state, and federal requirements for sanitation. Improper sanitation that results in client illness or skin reactions can put you out of business.

Don't Overdo It, But Too Little Is Often Too Little

If you have a large budget and you just want to put all the modalities in your day spa, that's fine. But also consider the fact that you want to offer new things from time to time. If you put all the equipment in at once, what will you add? In some situations it's better to plan your launches and stage the purchasing. If you know, for example, that you want to begin with a Vichy shower and add a hydrotherapy tub next year, you might do all the plumbing and tiling in advance and then just cover the floor of the hydrotherapy room with carpet or removable flooring in the meantime. Plumbing is a major expense and better done in advance if you plan to add equipment in the future. The electrical work and extra volume water heaters must be considered at this time as well. To have to tear out floors and plumb later is terribly expensive. If you are opening your day spa in a small space, it may not make sense to have too many hydrotherapy devices, particularly if the overall space can't accommodate the treatments following the water. If your space is really small, you can get the most out of just a shower, perhaps by adding a Swiss shower to the regular shower, and you will have increased the marketing effect of the same space.

If you are opening a new day spa or doing any construction on an existing space, to truly consider yourself a day spa you must put in a shower at the very least. Otherwise you are severely limited in treatments in a dry room with just sponges and a bowl of water. It isn't that most treatments can't be done, it's just ineffectual and time consuming. The cost and space for a shower will be well covered by the time and energy savings, not just from your standpoint but also from the client's.

Now a judgment call from your budget standpoint; if you can take a regular shower and make it a form of real hydrotherapy by installing a Swiss shower, will the additional few thousand dollars pay off in the long run for you? You may be in a position where you want to say yes and add the Swiss

"Be prepared to make $0 profit for the first 2–3 years. This is a labor-intensive business with high personnel costs. If you are an outstanding technician (esthetician, body therapist) but lack managerial experience, hire someone who knows how to run a small business. It's an investment you'll never regret."—Leah Kovitz, New Image By Leah, Tucson, Arizona

shower but the reality is that if you do, you run out of money for products. Then what is the best option. Most consultants would advise you to wait on the Swiss addition and put the money into the products because those products will in turn make cash for you to put back into the business. This is certainly the recommended avenue.

Quality Versus Price

I suppose everyone would have the very best car if money were no object. The reality, though, is that you will purchase the best car you possibly can within the financial framework you feel you can handle. This thinking will hold true for purchasing equipment for your day spa. In accounting terms, most of the major equipment for the spa is considered a capital expenditure. As such, great thought should be given to the longevity and quality desired. Because some of the equipment is large, if you consider using it for a long time, the difference in a few hundred dollars to upgrade to better equipment may not be an issue. But if the budget is very tight, every penny saved helps.

You will have the option of purchasing more but less expensive pieces of equipment versus less equipment of better quality for the same amount of money. This author cannot direct you on which route to go. You will have to make that decision. The important thing to remember is to compare apples with apples. It won't help you to be swayed by someone's lower price alone without considering the quality, warranties, education, and service. Certainly don't forget the negotiations on the education. Many spa owners jump for a cheaper price, sacrifice training, and in the end have to spend more than the difference to hire outside trainers when a little more at the beginning might have saved more money and hassle in the long run. Always remember, you get what you pay for.

. . . .

SPA POINT

Purchasing equipment, particularly hydrotherapy equipment, involves consideration of budget, space, goals, but also such practical subjects as proper sanitation and the time it takes to accomplish it, increased laundry requirements, and the staff to handle it. These are not inconsequential issues. They can cause problems among the staff and the sanitary practices can keep or lose a client. And don't sacrifice quality and education just for a cheaper model.

. . . .

CHECK LIST FOR DISCUSSIONS WITH SUPPLIERS
1. Hydrotherapy Tub: a) number of air and water jets (more is good)
                                                 b) power draining system, quick draining
                                                 c) manual massage hose included
                                                 d) nonstaining surface (seaweed, mud)

         e)   comfortable client fit
         f)   proper warranties
         g)   complete installation instructions
         h)   all parts included
         i)   manufacturer backup support
         j)   training
         k)   sanitation
         l)   contraindications

Pricing: high luxury market: $15,000–$30,000
              high middle market: $12,000–$16,000
              middle market: $ 8,000–$12,000

2. Whirlpool: a)   changing water and sanitation issues
                  b)   skin irritation potential
                  c)   professional appeal versus home use
                  d)   warranties
                  e)   installation and service
                  f)   contraindications

Author doesn't recommend whirlpools for day spas.

3. Inhalation Room: a)   cost versus usage
                  b)   overall spa balance
                  c)   products for inhalants
                  d)   installation, warranties, service
                  e)   sanitation
                  f)   contraindications

Pricing: Subject to plumbing and construction costs.

4. Steam Shower: a)   steam shower versus steam cabinet
                  b)   cost versus usage
                  c)   installation, warranties, service
                  d)   sanitation
                  e)   contraindications

Pricing: Subject to plumbing and construction costs.

5. Sauna: a)   day spa versus fitness center
                       applicability
                  b)   installation, warranties, service
                  c)   sanitation
                  d)   contraindications

Pricing: Prices subject to construction and electrical costs.

6. Scotch Hose: a)   space needed for distance, quick drain
                  b)   balance with other hydrotherapy
                  c)   installation, warranties, service
                  d)   training

e)   sanitation
f)   contraindications

Pricing: high luxury market: $5,000–$10,000
high middle market: $4,000–$ 6,000
middle market: $4,000–$ 6,000

7. Vichy Shower: a)   wet room required
b)   important to market treatments
c)   balance with other hydrotherapy
d)   water conserving heads, quick drain
e)   pulsations, hot to cold variation
f)   installation, warranties, service
g)   training, menu planning
h)   sanitation
i)   contraindications

Pricing: high luxury market: $5,000–$10,000
high middle market: $4,000–$ 6,000
middle market: $4,000–$ 6,000

8. Swiss Shower: a)   can install in regular shower
b)   water conserving heads, quick drain
c)   be sure shower has regular shower
head
d)   pulsations, hot to cold variation
e)   installation, warranties, service
f)   training, menu planning
g)   sanitation
h)   contraindications

Pricing: high luxury market: $5,000–$10,000
high middle market: $4,000–$ 6,000
middle market: $4,000–$ 6,000

9. Shower: a)   size and construction
b)   water conserving heads, quick drain
c)   installation, warranties, service
d)   sanitation
e)   contraindications

Pricing: Subject to plumbing and construction costs.

SOME COMBINATIONS ACCORDING TO MARKETS AND BUDGETS

The combinations listed are very general and not representative of all the possibilities. The listings are based on common combinations in the industry. Price ranges do not include room or finish out.

1. High Luxury Market:
   a) All equipment $50,000 plus
   b) Hydrotherapy tub, Vichy shower, Swiss shower, shower, Scotch hose, steam shower $25,000–$40,000
   c) Hydrotherapy tub, Vichy shower, Swiss shower, shower $20,000–$35,000

2. High Middle Market:
   a) Hydrotherapy tub, Vichy shower, Swiss shower, shower, Scotch hose, steam shower $25,000–$40,000
   b) Hydrotherapy tub, Vichy shower, Swiss shower, shower $20,000–$35,000
   c) Hydrotherapy tub, Vichy shower, shower $15,000–$25,000
   d) Vichy shower, Swiss shower, shower $10,000–$15,000

3. Middle Market:
   a) Hydrotherapy tub, Vichy shower, Swiss shower, shower $20,000–$35,000
   b) Vichy shower, Swiss shower, shower $10,000–$15,000
   c) Vichy shower, shower $5,000–$7,000
   d) Swiss shower, shower $5,000–$7,000
   e) Shower $1,000 plus.

· ·

SPA POINT

Equipment is a difficult issue because there are so many variables. It's prudent to keep budget in mind along with treatment goals, quality, and target market.

· ·

ACCESSORY EQUIPMENT AND SUPPLIES, PROFESSIONAL AND RETAIL

This is not a terribly expensive category but shouldn't be forgotten. The professional use items will not be expensive, but you should plan on a budget for a variety of accessories for retail as well. This category is often forgotten and when it comes time to open, there's no more liquid money for purchasing these things. Or by this time the spa owner feels nickelled and dimed to death and closes her mind to the purchase of the small things. The reality is that the accessories often provide additional cash income that can be quickly turned.

Accessory Equipment

Accessory equipment would include hydroculators, bolsters and pillows for beds, depilatory wax heaters, paraffin baths, electric heating masks/booties/mittens, wood lamps, electric bed warmers, bottle warmers, hot towel cabinets, OSHA compliant containers and supplies. The aggregate cost on all this equipment combined will normally run under $2,000. This category will not include the depilatory wax or refills for paraffin, just the equipment. The budget will be approximately the same for any of the three market categories. There are greater and lesser prices, obviously, but not significantly in comparison to the capital expenditures.

Accessory Products and Supplies

Professionally speaking, you will need items such as sheets, towels, blankets, comedone extractors, cotton, cotton tips, tissues, disinfectants and other OSHA compliant supplies, depilatory and paraffin waxes, and waxing supplies such as gloves, spatulas, and strips. You will need foil and plastic for body treatments (they run $2 to $4 per sheet), paper sheets for waxing, disposable applicators, mixing bowls and utensils, mask brushes, body exfoliation brushes, sponges, and skin shammies. Pricing can vary and your budget will depend on the number of rooms you plan to equip (Figure 4-6). As a rule of thumb, budget about $600–800 per room.

For retail you should have a sufficient supply of body brushes, sponges, skin shammies for both face and body, containers, makeup brushes, and other

FIGURE 4-6 *Accessory products are indispensable to the day spa.*

items that facilitate and enhance the sale of the cosmetics. You certainly want your clients using the proper tools to have a more effective treatment program. Why should you recommend a wash cloth when you don't sell one? As much as possible, you should be a one-stop retail center for all your client's cosmetic needs. Many spa owners lose out on this very profitable incremental business just because it's not part of the mainstream line. It's very important. Remember, if your client wants makeup sponges and goes to the department store to get them, likely as not the counter salesperson will attempt to sell cosmetics and you can lose out to a highly qualified retailer.

It is the strong opinion of this author that you must control all your clients' cosmetic and beauty-related purchases, perhaps with the exception of perfumes. They do not work well in a salon environment due to the fact that you normally wouldn't stock the tremendous variety a department store does and also because the consumer equates perfumes with the department store, hence the credibility isn't relative in the day spa. Some day spas do well with fragrance, but this isn't the norm.

It's difficult to set a budget for these accessory items because it depends on what and how many you choose to purchase. It may be sufficient to budget about $2,000, $1,000, and $500 respectively for high luxury, high middle, and middle markets. Please refer to *SalonOvations' In the Bag, Selling in the Salon* by Carol Phillips, an excellent resource for understanding your retailing responsibilities and capabilities. According to Phillips, "For you to distance yourself from the competition you do not have to perform one task 1,000 times better. You perform 1,000 tasks 1 percent better. Will your effort pay off? Carlzon, the President of SAS, was able to take an $8 million loss into a $71 million moneymaker in less than one year concentrating on the details." In other words, don't ignore the small accessories. Even they can and will make a difference.

• •

SPA POINT

Accessories are just as important as your major purchases and often left to the last minute when the budget or inclination to buy is gone. Budget for this from the beginning to prevent it from becoming a sore subject at the end.

• •

Synopsis

There are too many variables in each person's situation to be able to present specific dollars or purchasing requirements. The rough categorization is based on the fact that this author believes day spas are a middle class and above market, and that you must use professional equipment and products throughout. You may not be able to purchase and develop all you want in the beginning, but there is tremendous room for growth. You can start in the middle market and end up in the high luxury market, or you can start and stay in the high middle market. You are in the business driver's seat, but don't do it all alone. Solicit the advice and counsel of professionals, from other day spa owners who have been down the road you're going to professional consultants, accountants, and attorneys. Take your time and base all your purchasing on a well-developed business plan.

Review

1. Why is purchasing such a critical part of the day spa development?

2. Why is it important to know clearly why you want to open a day spa?

3. What is one advantage of working with a professional consultant?

4. What are the three markets for day spas used in this chapter?

5. Discuss two important factors of choosing suppliers.

6. What are the two major channels of distribution and which one is most common for the day spa market?

7. What are four considerations for choosing product lines? Discuss one of your choice.

8. What are two considerations when purchasing equipment? Discuss one of your choice.

9. Should accessory equipment and supplies be programmed into your budget? If so, why?

CHAPTER 5
Financing the Day Spa

OVERVIEW

Perhaps the most difficult subject to address in any book, money and finance become the defining factor in the entire business. We always hear, it takes money to make money. This author agrees. There are times when spending more is better, and times when it isn't. We will look a bit at financing issues, but to really understand business and money you will need to look at business books and take business courses. The subject cannot be covered well within the scope of this book. Your major accounting and financing issues should be discussed with your accountant, attorney, consultant, and advisers. A few tips are in order to help you understand some business concepts related to opening a day spa. The discussion herein is brief and not designed to replace professional direction or business experience.

GENERAL DAY SPA BUSINESS UNDERSTANDING

Banks

"Start small and add. Begin with tried and true treatments and then educate the regulars you acquire to new and more exciting treatments. Let the guest/client be a part of your growth so they take ownership of your business and feel your success as theirs as you grow. That way they'll remain loyal."—Marguerite Rivel, Spa Director, The Broadmoor, Colorado Springs

It's great if you have the money to finance all the expenses related to opening a day spa. That's certainly the ideal situation but unfortunately is not applicable to most people desirous of opening a spa. Therefore, financing from an outside source may be necessary. You must know that in today's banking climate, the beauty industry is not well thought of. If you walk into an unknown bank and ask for a loan to start a salon or day spa you should anticipate a rather negative reaction, even if the bank officer doesn't show it. The default experience with salons is great, which naturally makes the banks a little hesitant. This does not mean it's impossible to obtain financing; it simply means you must work harder to present a professional, well-put-together business plan to convince the bank that you're a fairly safe risk. We'll discuss a few points about this business plan later but suffice it to say here that you must be able to show effectively how you will pay the bank back in such a manner as to make the bank feel at ease, since this isn't the normal tendency.

It's also advisable to work with known bankers. If you are already in business and plan to open the day spa down the road, it's vital to develop a personal trusting relationship now. You may even want to borrow a small amount of money now and pay it back quickly just to build a track record. It helps when a bank has a good repayment history on you. Even if you don't really need a loan now, the interest you will pay may have important long-term relationship-building value. It's a small but good investment.

It's also valuable to keep the bank informed of the status of your business by sending quarterly financial statements along with notes updating your progress. The quality and stability of your history with a bank is very helpful when you go for that big loan.

Small Business Administration

The Small Business Administration (SBA) is another avenue of potential financing. The SBA most often works closely with financial institutions and banks to guarantee loans, so you will still work with a bank or financial institution. There is normally a lot of paperwork to prepare an SBA application (often called *package*). The paperwork is tedious but valuable because it really helps you think out your business plan, goals, and repayment concepts and is helpful for developing a good business head. If you are accepted, you may even obtain a slightly better rate of interest, although this is no longer guaranteed.

If you choose to go the SBA route, or your bank advises it, work closely with the proper authorities to make the package as complete and realistic as possible. Some prospective day spa owners make totally unrealistic projections that come back to haunt them when it doesn't work out. Remember, the SBA will be following your progress through regular financial statements. It's much better for you to be realistic, particularly if you ever want to go back to the SBA for expansion loans. Be honest, realistic, and positive. Don't paint a worst-case scenario, but don't overexaggerate either.

The SBA also offers seminars and information to help you understand how it works. You may find this information in the business and government pages of your phone book.

Outside Investors

There are two types of venture capitalists: those who search out new interesting businesses and those who might support you because they know and believe in you. If you know the investor, you may not need to put together a business plan. However, it's better if you approach your known investor in a very businesslike manner and complete the same formal business plan. It will serve to build confidence and interest in your project, and it helps organize you and keep you on track.

An unknown investor will, of course, require a business plan. Venture capitalists want to know the bottom line, just as a bank does, but they are often very interested in the romance of the project as well. For this type of investor, it's good to enhance and be more detailed about some of your philosophical strategy. The bank is less interested in this aspect of the business.

DO YOU REALLY INTEND TO PAY BACK YOUR LOAN?

As we are all aware, in today's world bankruptcy is rampant; shirking loans and business responsibility is commonplace. A word to the wise: don't do it. When you sit down and take pencil in hand to develop your business plan, is your attitude one of, "Oh, well if it doesn't work I'll just close the door and do something else"? Or is it, "No matter what, I'm going to make this business work"? Whether it's your money or someone else's, you must open your day spa with the attitude of absolutely making it work. You must know that you will pay every single penny back. This will not only protect the lender, but ensure in your own mind that you really are serious about what you're doing. It will guard your spending and make you think as a businessperson, not as an artist.

Every time a salon or day spa goes broke and declares bankruptcy, it affects us all. It makes the banks, financial institutions, and investors skeptical. It hurts the next professional and our image, relegates our profession to a trade, and contributes to the negative image we are all trying to change. And most of all, it hurts you. Please remember to ask yourself as you begin to put a business plan together whether you are really ready to do this. Do you feel strongly enough to put your own personal guarantee on a loan? Do you believe without a shadow of a doubt that you can make a go of it? If you cannot answer yes then you aren't ready to start your own business. If you truly can answer yes then you have a good chance for success because you absolutely can make it work if you want to.

THE BUSINESS PLAN

There are many ways in which to write a good business plan. There are also numerous ways to present it. It's recommended that it be typed and in some kind of presentation format. Photos, drawings, and graphics all contribute to the impression the lender will have. Your consultant, accountant, and attorney will all be able to assist you in the proper presentation format. The following represents some of the subjects you may want to include in the business plan.

By the way, even if you have all the funds yourself, you may still want to go though the exercise of developing a written business plan. It will certainly help keep you on track. A note of caution: for reasons unknown, your accountant or bank may request a different format, different information, or expanded information. Follow their specific guidelines.

Parts of the Business Plan

INTRODUCTION
Give a brief history of how the desire came to be. Why do you want to open a day spa and why do you want to borrow money?

MISSION STATEMENT
The mission statement states in a nutshell what you believe about your business. It tells your client and anyone else who you are. If you don't know how to develop a mission statement, research various company's mission statements. You may think you're too small in comparison to Sears or Wal-Mart, but the reality is that you are a company too. The mission statement goes a long way with your own clients and employees. Later, you may even want to print it on a plaque to hang in your day spa or include it in your literature.

BACKGROUND HISTORY
This section covers your professional background and the history of your company. This is a section representing your professional credibility and perhaps what makes you uniquely qualified to open this business.

THE NEW OPERATION

This section backs up your mission statement and states what the new business will be. It's good to include information on anything that makes your day spa unique. This will include significant aspects of the operation.

MANAGEMENT AND STAFFING

Who is the day spa? You will want to provide brief résumés on your management team if applicable. You may want to discuss your operational management system—employees or independent contractors. You should give brief job descriptions of the various positions, particularly for the management team.

YOUR COMPANY AND MANAGEMENT STRENGTH

This section also discusses what makes you different from a personnel standpoint as well as from a mission standpoint. In other words, why do you feel your day spa will be successful?

COMPETITION

You should openly discuss the potential competition and how you plan to be successful in view of it. There is always competition, but it can be an added incentive and good challenge to your success. Competition causes you to be better and increases demand in the marketplace. Show how this will be a positive in your business.

These first seven items are important for both banks and investors. Be brief for the banks and enlarge for the investors. The next section is the meat of the business plan.

FINANCIAL PROJECTIONS

Revenue

You should project your revenues for a period of at least two to five years. Be realistic, not negative or overly optimistic. Be sure your revenue capability more than covers the pay back on the loan. You may want to consider at least a triple revenue to expense balance. Check with your accountant on this for the ratio varies greatly depending on the financing and goals. A computer can be very helpful to extend the projections over the five-year period. You will definitely need your accountant's help for this section. This is a very important part of the whole financial picture. Take your time and do it correctly.

Expenses

You will want to balance the revenue projections with expense projections. Obviously you must show the capability to more than pay back the loan. The time frame for both revenue and expenses should be the same. Some prefer to show the loan request in this section, but it may be better to present it by itself in its own category.

LOAN REQUEST AND EXPENSE PROJECTIONS

The lender certainly must know how much you plan to borrow and what you plan to spend it on. Some lenders will lend you a lump sum and some will

"Now I've lived through all of this I know I would have put an equal amount of importance on the management/business, figure tracking side as I did on the technical part of being an esthetician."—David Miller, David & Mary's, Indianapolis

create a line of credit on which you can draw. This means that, for example, a line of credit for $100,000 is agreed upon. When you need funds you will draw a check from the bank or investor against that total amount. You haven't actually borrowed the whole $100,000 but parts of it. This is good because you have to consider when you want to ask for money, and you also aren't responsible for paying interest on the whole amount, just the actual borrowed part. Sometimes this line of credit helps prevent overly easy spending.

Some loans must be done on a lump sum basis, in which case you'd better put the money in the bank and watch your spending. When you decide the amount you want to borrow, be cautious. Don't borrow tons more than you need, but don't underestimate either. In most cases, you will wind up spending more than you originally intended, so a bit of padding for safety is important. If you have a little money left over, you can always put it in a bank account for reserve against the unexpected or begin paying the loan back a little early. Early to prompt payment is always impressive to the lender.

ASSETS
In the financial presentation, you should also show any fixed assets you take to the project. In this case we're talking about real property assets, not your CIDESCO International Diploma.

REPAYMENT PLAN
This should be a brief statement about how you would like to repay the loan. Include any specifics such as desired payments and prepayment potential. (Be aware of balloon clauses where the financial institution has an option for a large or complete final payment at any point in the loan.)

CLOSING/GOALS/COMMENTS
This is a closing section, a chance for you to "close the sale." In other words, this is where you tell the lender/investor why their money is secure in you, why you will do a great job, why this is a wonderful opportunity for them. Keep this section somewhat short and don't embellish. Sound positive, professional, and businesslike. And finally, ask for the loan or investment.

. . . .

SPA POINT
The business plan is not only essential for obtaining financing but also vital for your own business control and understanding. The business plan will help you organize your thoughts and keep you on track. It forces you to think like a businessperson, and it's critical for obtaining any financing no matter what the source. You should write a business plan even if you don't need financing and have all the money in the world, if you're serious about your business success, that is. And finally, never open a day spa or borrow money if you don't really have a strong intent and confidence to make it succeed.

. . . .

Synopsis

Purchasing is, of course, the most critical phase of the spa development. You must know your target market, develop a budget, and work with professionals who really know what they're doing. The esthetic business operates differently from the hair distribution channels and can be confusing and frustrating. Often it's wise to seek the advice of professional spa consultants. But be sure the consultant you choose had truly had developmental experience beyond just having worked in one. Choosing your product lines and equipment again involves a clear understanding of your goals. But the stability, delivery, service, training, and backup are sometimes more important than the products themselves. Keep a balance and check out the potential companies for their industry reputation.

Review

1. List three topics that need to be addressed in a business plan and discuss one in detail.

CHAPTER 6
Strategic Development of the Day Spa _____

OVERVIEW

This is an exciting chapter because the actual day spa will begin to develop here. It's impossible to cover all the variables within the scope of this book, but discussions will once again be based on the concept of the three markets—high luxury market, high middle market, and middle market. Since we do not have specific budgets to work with within these categories, all discussions will be based on general guidance for day spa development.

DESIGNERS AND ARCHITECTS

If you are quite creative and have an interior design or architectural background you may be highly qualified to design and develop your own day spa. However, most likely you don't or you wouldn't be in the day spa business. As a result, it is advisable to obtain the services of a designer and/or architect. If, however, you've worked in a number of day spa situations and have a clearcut idea of what you want to do, you may just need to have a draftsperson do your layouts. You may wind up being your own best general contractor. Some of the manufacturers of major spa and salon equipment also provide design services that can help you develop the layout and blueprints but usually do not have the personal rapport and expertise of a specialized day spa designer.

If you do not have extensive day spa experience and you don't want to make a lot of costly or disastrous mistakes, it is prudent to seek the advice of professional designers and architects. The trick to obtaining this advice is to find someone with specific day spa or salon experience. Thousands upon thousands of dollars have been lost in good intentions due to lack of proper experience in this field. If the person you are considering has no experience in this field, it would be wise to search a little farther. The sample layouts in this chapter are presented by Ms. Diana Drake, owner of RBD Interiors in Dallas, a person with extensive salon and day spa design and space-planning expertise. These sample layouts are very general and not specifically designed for you to use. You must develop your own layout according to the specifications relative to your space.

"SPA SPYING"

In previous chapters you have been advised to visit other day spas and talk to the owners. This can be a wonderful avenue of information, but at times it can be problematical if that spa owner views you as competition and gives you erroneous information or no information. In some instances, it's easier to obtain openness and information from a day spa in another city. It is well worth your investment in time and money to visit day spas and sample services from a variety of styles and scales. Each time take notes, ask questions, and be honest about who you are. If you are "spying," you may think you're being clever enough that the owner or technician doesn't know who you are. The reality is that we can usually tell just by the way you act or questions you inevitably ask. Then you lose out because the "spying" is a turnoff to friendly help. Certainly there are times when everyone in this profession has played the role of "mystery shopper," but as a rule it's not the best approach. Most spa owners are happy to share information. A client of mine, Mrs. Ginny Burge, owner of Day Spa Beautique Salon, stated, "When I visit with people who come to see my operation, I share my sources with them because I know how hard it was for me to find sources when I put my day spa in, and I know that you can't list specific sources in your book."

A further recommendation; when you go out there to "pick brains" and receive warm open assistance, remember how helpful that was to you when someone visits you later. It is this author's opinion that nobody loses by sharing. Competition that is healthy is good for everyone in the area. Nobody will develop the business the way you did anyway. You are totally unique. It's up to you to keep growing on your own, and you don't have to worry about someone else taking anything away from you.

· ·

SPA POINT

It is often instinct to try to save money by doing it yourself. However, in an enterprise of such importance, in-depth research, spa visitation, and the employment of professionals in their field may save you much more money and heartache in the long run. There are innumerable variables; if you are not highly experienced, you need outside professional help.

· ·

DAY SPA DEVELOPMENT

Location

Probably the most critical issue at the outset is the amount of square footage and location. As has been said over and over again in all business books, the crux of the business is location, location, location. Within the confines of your city or area, the location will be vitally important. The choice of location type is a big decision. Do you want to open your spa in an office building, a shopping center, a mall, or in a quaint storefront property on the main street in town? Do you want to buy land and build your own salon? It is, of course, more difficult and costly to purchase land and build, but if you do that you have more flexibility and a good property investment.

Other issues related to the location will include zoning requirements and limitations, parking requirements and limitations, signage (some places have very strict restrictions on signs), local regulations, licensure, construction codes, and labor unions. Imagine spending $200,000 on a fabulous new day spa and two weeks after you put up a $5,000 sign finding out that signs are not allowed. And what about the competition in the area? Is it a plus or sufficiently worrisome that you should consider another area? This could be a serious setback. All of these issues should be checked out at the time you are choosing the location.

Another issue you must know about is how the space rental is handled. Is it a certain amount of money per month or a rent plus a percentage of retail sales? There are many variations and this is always negotiable to some extent. If you're planning to be very strong in retail, take that into consideration. In most malls and shopping centers, percentage of retail is commonplace. If you don't want anyone knowing your figures, you'll need to negotiate something else if it's possible. In most lease properties, the owner has a budget to assist you in finish out, but if you don't ask, you won't get it. It's usually quite a negotiable point.

There are commercial realtors who will do a lot of this negotiating for you. Be sure the realtor is working for you not the property.

. . . .

SPA POINT

The location of your day spa has a great deal to do with the success potential. Remember location, location, location! In any retail business, location can make or break you. Choose well.

. . . .

Demographics

When considering the location, you must do some demographic research. Demographics refers to the characteristics of the population in the area (i.e., families, genders, and income levels). This information is often available through the chamber of commerce and real estate companies. It's vitally important to be sure the demographics suit the market you want to draw. The larger the city, the smaller the client draw you should expect because of other day spas that likely exist, unless you are extremely well known. If you open a new unknown day spa, don't expect people to drive one hour across the city to visit it regularly. On the other hand, if you have the only day spa in town your geographic area may be larger. If your intent is to develop a high luxury market day spa, don't put it in the industrial area of town. It needs to be accessible to the chosen market.

. . . .

SPA POINT

Demographics are an important tool to determine if your location is beneficial to the market to which you want to cater. Do not make the mistake of just jumping into a location without researching the demographics of the area.

. . . .

Square Footage

How large a space do you want? How many rooms, how many hair and nail stations do you plan to have? Do you want a large waiting and retail area or just a small one? Will you allow space for an employee lounge and office?

"Overall square footage can be modified to almost any size. You need rheostatic lights, soothing music throughout, lots of soft artwork and cool relaxing colors. There should be water (hot and cold) in every room, sinks in all treatment rooms, showers, and, if baths, oversized pipes and water heaters."—Marguerite Rivel, Spa Director, The Broadmoor, Colorado Springs

These are all critical questions to consider while you're dreaming about your ideal day spa and then again realistically when you know what the overall square footage of the chosen space will be. Your rent is normally based upon the square footage. And then you will have development/construction costs that could vary from as little as $35 per square foot to more than $100 per square foot. The determinant of square foot finish out depends on the area and construction costs in that area along with the quality and luxury of what you plan to construct. This is again where your three markets play a critical role.

Although it's impossible to say how much you should spend per square foot, the following might be a guideline for some general square foot sizes in each category. But remember, you can have a very high luxury day spa in a small space and vice versa. It will depend entirely on how many rooms, whether your day spa will offer only esthetics or include hair and nails, wet and dry areas, staff space, and retail and reception areas. The generalities for square footage and cost per square foot are based somewhat on the sample layouts shown throughout this chapter in a typical metropolitan area.

MARKET	SQUARE FOOTAGE	COST PER SQUARE FOOT
High luxury market:	4,000 square feet plus	$100 plus
High middle market:	2,000–4,000 square feet	$50–$75
Middle market:	850–2,000 square feet	$35–$50

NOTE: *In middle market, $35–$50 doesn't include wet room costs, which are necessarily higher.*

PLAN FOR GROWTH

As you will see in a few of the experts' quotes interspersed throughout the book, a common problem encountered is not allowing space for growth. You should choose your location and space with some thought of future growth. You may not use all the space initially, but it's wise to at least consider how you plan to grow as the business prospers. Obviously you don't want to pay for unused space, but you also have the problem of higher costs later, for plumbing and electrical work. Some locations may be chosen based upon space options as the business grows. Whether you are building your own building or leasing, consider the fact that most construction done is difficult to take with you when you decide to move or expand. So growth potential is a viable issue when developing your day spa. And you should assume that you will grow. Let's hope you do anyway!

· ·

SPA POINT

Almost all costs related to rent, construction, and finish out come back to the square footage. Choosing your location and determining your square footage will give you a good idea of budgetary considerations. If you are developing an upscale image, always allow enough square footage for client comfort. Also, do not overlook the growth potential when choosing your space. If you do your job well, growth will come.

· ·

CONSTRUCTION
Wet Versus Dry Areas

Usually, the most expensive areas in a day spa are the wet areas, just as the hydrotherapy equipment is the largest equipment expense. If you're renovating an empty space or building from scratch, the wet areas must weigh heavily in your space planning, square footage, and budget. Unless you just happen to have tons of money, you will need to give serious consideration to the number of wet rooms.

First of all, let's define what we mean by wet versus dry area. A wet room simply means a room that is designed to be able to get wet. It's normally a tiled (or other similar water-resistant material) room with a floor drain. Cementuous board is required behind tile (and is expensive). Water-resistant wall is called greenboard. A dry room is one that should not get wet. A dry room has normal sheet rock walls and floor coverings. Massages and facial treatments are most often done in dry rooms whereas a hydrotherapy tub or Vichy shower mud or seaweed treatment is normally done in a wet room.

If you put a number of showers in wet areas, these may constitute multiple wet rooms or one large wet room. There are a number of variations, but it's recommended that each major hydrotherapy modality (tub, Vichy shower) be placed in a wet room of it's own. A regular shower and Swiss shower can be built within the same shower space, but beyond that each one should be individual. As such, if you decided that you wanted three hydrotherapy tub rooms and two Vichy shower rooms, you are looking at the cost for five wet rooms just for the two modalities.

Some day spas build one large wet room and include both the tub and Vichy shower in that one room to save money. This can certainly be done, but the negative to this is the issue of privacy. Unless a couple, sisters, or friends take treatments together, you will tie up the room for only one person. This is not cost effective. If you feel that two strangers should be in that room at the same time, think again. Most American consumers are still too modest for this openness, particularly in the upscale market. It's far preferable to have one room per tub or Vichy shower.

As stated previously, the Swiss shower fits inside a normal shower (4' × 4' is preferable to the smaller 3' × 3') anyway so to combine an overhead shower with the Swiss shower is normal and quite cost effective. A questionable issue lies with the Scotch hose if you want one. The Scotch hose requires a distance of 8–12 feet for ideal treatment. To construct a special wet area just for this is expensive. It's not the most popular treatment currently so it may be advisable to install it in the same room with the hydrotherapy tub or Vichy shower. It will be impossible to do two people at the same time, but may be more cost effective overall.

> NOTE: *A very critical thing not to forget is the need for a very large water heater or boiler (100 gallon) or even two due to the high water consumption with the wet rooms, facial rooms, hair areas, laundry, bathrooms, and the like.*

WET ROOMS

The cost of building a wet room is high. Broad averages place the per-square-footage cost at a minimum of $50–$75 and as high as $150 ($100 plus is realistic in metropolitan areas). Remember, this doesn't include the hydrotherapy equipment. It's just the wet room construction. The square footage needed for a Vichy shower is a little smaller than for a hydrotherapy tub.

Vichy Shower Wet Room:	9' × 12' to 10' × 12'
Hydrotherapy Tub Room:	12' × 12' to 12' × 14'

The actual sizes may depend slightly on the size of your Vichy shower table or tub. But consider a space of at least 3 feet on all sides of the table or tub. As such, there won't be much of a cost difference between the three markets. Minor variables may include the quality of the lighting and price of tile. In any case you're looking at $15,000 to $20,000 per room not counting the equipment.

If you're not going to have separate rooms for the Vichy shower and the tub, the question becomes, which is more important? This is often difficult to answer because it depends on the overall budget, the treatment goals, and the projected usage of each. Some experts feel that the Vichy shower is better because it's more versatile, the shower treatment by itself as well as various exfoliating and wraps that can be done in the Vichy shower room. On the other hand, the hydrotherapy tub itself offers the ultimate in hydrotherapy, particularly if you have the underwater hose for massage. The ideal would be to have both, but the wet room cost must not be forgotten. You will have to make your own choice or follow the advice of your consultant. The target market and overall appeal may determine the number of wet rooms and designate whether it's more luxury or more basic.

Two things that are critical for the wet room are a shower hose for hosing down the walls and floor and perfect drain placement and sloping. The hose can also be used for rinsing the client, but it's an important time saver for cleaning the room. The power of the spray is also important to speed up the cleaning process. Be sure, however, that it's a comfortable intensity for the client, because the client will not view it as a device for cleaning the room.

If the room isn't well sloped to the drain and it takes a long time to clear the water off the floor, it will seriously slow down the process of getting the next client in the room. Be absolutely certain that the construction is well done and the room drains well. Test it several times long before construction people sign off the project and leave. Absolutely do not take a chance on a homemade job. There can be real drainage problems in tall buildings with multiple floors as well. Check into this. If you are leasing, be sure you have already checked with the lessor regarding core drilling into the slab for drainage before you sign a lease.

There are wall textures and paint that are water resistant so in some cases day spa owners choose not to completely tile the room. If you plan to tile part of the wall, be sure you've tiled up the wall at least 6 feet. Be sure that whatever the walls and ceiling are constructed of can withstand a hose-down several times a day. Hopefully anticipate ten to twenty clients per day.

Tile floors can be very slippery, even if the client is wearing foot coverings, sandals, or paper slippers. It is imperative that you choose textured or mosaic tiles that help resist slippage. This reduces the risk of a client falling.

Colors and lighting should be relaxing and comfortable to the eyes. Lights should be on dimmer switches so that the technician can reduce lighting during the treatment but have sufficiently bright lighting for applications. Also, you need to have all electrical source's in wet areas well protected from water. Do not use very cold colors in a wet room. Psychologically it may chill the client. You want to maintain a warm, comfortable feel but not too feminine if you're catering to both sexes.

A wet room needs to be well ventilated to avoid the feeling of stuffiness or mildew accumulation. It's nice to have a window or skylight in the room to give an open feeling.

> *"You must know the amperage and wattage output of all equipment to give the electrician so that you have separate fuse boxes. Also you must protect all electrical sources from water. You must know your plumbing equipment and how much water is needed at all times for the laundry, tub, and shower to be going all at the same time."* —
> Annette Hanson, Atelier Esthetique, New York

. . . .

SPA POINT

The wet room is the greatest cost factor in a day spa, but you must have some hydrotherapy and body treatment to be a true day spa. Planning your wet areas carefully in conjunction with your target market and overall goals will help you determine what hydrotherapy services to offer and how many wet rooms you will need.

. . . .

DRY ROOMS

Dry rooms are the treatment rooms where there is no need for tiling or water resistance. Even in a dry room, however, having a sink is preferable. Since all rooms need cabinets anyway, a small compact sink with a tall faucet will suffice.

Facial Rooms

Facial rooms need several 4-plex electrical outlets for equipment positioned on the floor, in cabinets, or on a power bar underneath the cabinet kick plate. There should also be a couple of 4-plex outlets on the counter. It's better to have too much electrical capability than too little, as well as more cabinets than you think you will need. Facial rooms must have sinks with both hot and cold running water. Be sure the cabinets can close and even lock. Additionally, the lighting should be controlled by dimmer switches, both by the door at the entrance of the room and also near the technician's working area. It's much better for the esthetician to be able to dim the lights from the treatment position than to have to stop and walk back across the room. The room itself should be a comfortable size depending on what is being done. Keep the equipment in mind when determining the size (chair, steamer, machine, trolley). For a more luxury clientele, be sure the rooms aren't too small. It may take a bit more space but roominess is more comfortable for the client.

RECOMMENDED ROOM SIZES

High luxury market:	10' × 12' or 10' × 10'
High middle market:	10' × 10' or 8' × 10'
Middle market:	8' × 10' or 7' × 9'

FINISH OUT COSTS

High luxury market:	$40–$60 per square foot
High middle market:	$30–$40 per square foot
Middle market:	$20–$30 per square foot

Be sure the chair or bed will fit into the smaller spaces along with equipment, particularly depending on whether the technician will sit or stand. If the room is 7' × 9', you must be creative in constructing fold-out shelves and high but narrow cabinets to give the illusion of space and yet work efficiently. The ideal size if being used for both massage and facials is about 10' × 10'.

You may wonder why there would be a difference in room sizes for the three different markets. It's because of the cost per square foot to finish it out as well as for rent or mortgage payments. Large, airy space is better, but it's not impossible to develop a very nice small spa with very little square footage. Diana Drake once developed a very attractive small skin care salon in only 300 square feet and was able somehow to create two treatment areas, a makeup station (actually constructed on a door) and a retail/reception area. It was incredibly well done.

When putting in small rooms, often the owner chooses to mirror a wall or two to give the illusion of a larger size. It does give this illusion, but there's a negative to this as well. Any time there is a mirror in a facial room, the client will be more prone to stay longer in the room after the treatment than you desire. She may put on her makeup, gaze at the results of the treatment, or just plain dawdle. This is not good because you want the room vacated as soon as possible so that you can get the next client in.

> *"Special warm lighting is needed as it creates ambiance in the service area. We have light music—no mood music—as it seems to relate to more people."—* Ginny Burge, Day Spa Beautique Salon, Houston, Texas

Massage Rooms

Massage rooms are normally dry rooms, but massage can, of course, be done in a wet room as well. The good part about building a massage room the same size as a facial room and with a sink and cabinets is that the rooms can be used for facials and waxing if necessary. Also remember that if your day spa is busy, you will do well to have the flexibility of being able to do some body treatments in those rooms, and a sink for rinsing sponges and filling bowls is vital. Many body treatments can be done in a massage room if all the wet rooms are being used. Massage rooms must have dimmer switches, preferably at both ends of the room for ease of technician accessibility.

Many day spas have tiny massage rooms, just big enough for the technician to slip around the table. The negative to this is a very closed-in claustrophobic sensation for the client as well as the technician. A roomier space is conducive to more repeat business and staff peace. The expense is worthwhile if you can manage it. Sizes really don't vary much from facial rooms. Smaller massage rooms can also double for waxing rooms, and at least one or two waxing rooms are imperative. Don't forget, waxing is one of your most profitable services so don't ignore the space for it.

ROOM SIZES

High luxury market:	10' × 10'
High middle market:	10' × 10', 8' × 10'
Middle market:	10' × 10', 8' × 10', 7' × 9'

FINISH OUT COSTS
WILL NOT VARY MUCH IN EACH MARKET

High luxury market:	$25–$35 per square foot
High middle market:	$20–$30 per square foot
Middle market:	$15–$20 per square foot

· ·

SPA POINT

The dry rooms will be used for facial treatments, waxing, and massage. These rooms do not have to be elaborate, and the flexibility of overlapping the services is advantageous. Therefore, it's suggested that you put sinks with hot and cold running water in all treatment rooms. By doing so you do not limit your treatment capability.

· ·

PUBLIC AREAS

This is the category that represents the entry, makeup, retail, and reception areas, staff lounge, changing rooms, laundry areas, hallways, bathrooms, offices, and storage. There are endless variables in this category. The following represent some generalities that you should consider.

- In a more upscale day spa, you will want to designate a special place for the client to have consultations and lunches (with spa packages).

- Bathrooms nowadays must be constructed (and rightly so) for the handicapped. Check local codes for requirements.

- In a larger day spa with a lot of traffic, it's advisable to separate the check-in reception area from the check-out area. If the area is the same and it's crowded, clients will often want to get out of the crowd and the retail sales opportunity may be lost. Additionally, crowds cause confusion for the receptionist and telephone staff and you never want this to happen. The telephone contact is the most important in the entire spa. If the telephone person is overworked and stressed out, the quality of telephone impression will suffer.

- Do not skimp on your retail display presentation. The greatest income in your day spa is through retail so the retail design and development is critical. Always allot a sufficient amount in your budget to build or install high-quality, well-lit displays.

- The owner/manager should have an office.

- Be sure to allow an area for your staff to eat and rest. If there is no place for the staff, they will hang out at the front desk and this causes tremendous problems, not to mention being unprofessional looking and disturbing the telephone staff. Naturally the office and staff areas do not have to be as elegant as the client areas, but dropping down too much gives a very poor image to your staff (you never want to give the staff the impression that they are less important to you).

- You need to consider telephones for employees and clients to use (lock out long distance) away from the front desk, but not in the staff lounge where they can easily be monopolized.

- If you have a large space, you should also have a couple of commercial size and strength washers and dryers because the laundry in body spa treatments is extensive.

- Take into account the importance of quality lighting and sound. Use a lot of well-directed spot lighting, particularly on displays. You should have very nice fixtures and dimmer switches in all treatment areas. Electricity is a substantial part of the cost. Walls, particularly in the quiet areas, must specifically be sound insulated. Be careful about grids and return air ducts, particularly in the dropped ceilings and between treatment rooms. You cannot have sound transferring between rooms.

- You should have a good-quality sound system. The nicer the spa, the more important the quality of music. A jam box with tapes is fine for a small middle market salon, but a music system is better for a fine facility. There are music subscription services available that can gear specific types of music to the different areas of the spa. As an example, you may want louder, bouncier music in the hair area, but quieter more soothing music in the massage area. Clashes in music in a day spa can be a very great problem.

- Plants in a day spa add a great deal to the ambiance. Mixing silk plants with real plants works well.

- Another controversial concept is the positioning of the services. Should the hair department be located in the front or in the back? This is a matter of choice. However, as the day spa evolves, the concentration on body is predominant. Additionally, in hair and nails, you will have to deal with chemical odors (see your OSHA regulations on this) to some extent. Your spa design should take this into consideration.

- The mood and decor are a personal issue. However, you must determine if you want your day spa to cater only to women or to men as well. Your decoration and colors will be important depending on to whom you will cater. The quality of accessories, fixtures, materials, and fabrics will be determined by the target market. As with all types of businesses, be somewhat cautious about being too tied to your own tastes. If you want a broad-based clientele, neutrals and subtlety are advisable.

- Be absolutely certain to place the public areas, which are normally noisier, away from the quiet areas.

Some rough estimates on square footage costs are listed, but remember that this can be anything in reality depending on what you're offering. Seek the advice of your designer for more specific cost estimates.

"Lighting: white light in makeup area, soft lighting in facial, massage, pedicure, and manicure area, then ample light in body treatment areas for application then dimmers for rest time. Sound: speaker in all rooms for soft relaxing music conducive to relaxation." —Lynn Kirkpatrick, With Class, A Day Spa, Tyler, Texas

High luxury market:	$30–$50 per square foot
High middle market:	$20–$30 per square foot
Middle market:	$15–$25 per square foot

. . . .

SPA POINT

Designing the public areas is a very enjoyable part of the process. This is where creativity and decor are most appreciated. However, issues of crowds, noise, sufficient retail display, staff areas, and offices require tremendous thought. The entry, reception, and client areas must be comfortable and conducive to doing business. You must also avoid overt eclectic taste if you want to cater to a broad-based population.

. . . .

LICENSES, REGULATIONS, ZONING, AND OSHA

Although this isn't a particularly fun subject, you cannot overlook the fact that your local, state, and federal authorities play a role in your business.

DETAILS FOR UPPER LUXURY DAY SPA—4,400 SQUARE FOOT

Spa Includes:

4 Facial rooms

4 Massage rooms

2 Wax rooms

1 Vichy shower with "room" hose, standard shower and glass block window, walls and floor tiled

1 Hydrotherapy room with "room" hose, standard shower, tiled walls and floor

Changing room with 6 half lockers, hanging hooks, and bench with hamper below

1 Swiss shower with dry-off area

1 Standard shower with dry-off area

1 Small restroom

Seating for 2-skylight overhead

Planters and display

1 Washer, 1 Dryer, 1 Water heater

Emergency exit

Mini "inner" courtyard, lights via glass block, 3 separate rooms

1 Drying table

1 Waiting

Storage closet

Display case

Public Areas Include:

Check-in desk with computer terminal and 42"-high client counter

Waiting for 8 with phone for client

Check-out counter with computer terminal

Client coat closet

Makeup table for 2

Retail area with displays

Restroom with handicap facilities

Office

Planters

Courtyard with seating for 8, waterfall with pond

Employee area:

1 Washer

1 Dryer

1 Water heater

Employee lockers and coat hooks

Seating for 9

Kitchen—dishwasher and refrigerator

Employee restroom

Employee entrance

Cabinet for folding and storage

Hair Includes:

8 Hair stations

3 Shampoo stations

2 Hair dryers

2 Waiting

Changing room with 6 half lockers and bench with hamper below

Mixing room

Storage closet

Nails Includes:

4 Manicure Stations

2 Pedicure rooms

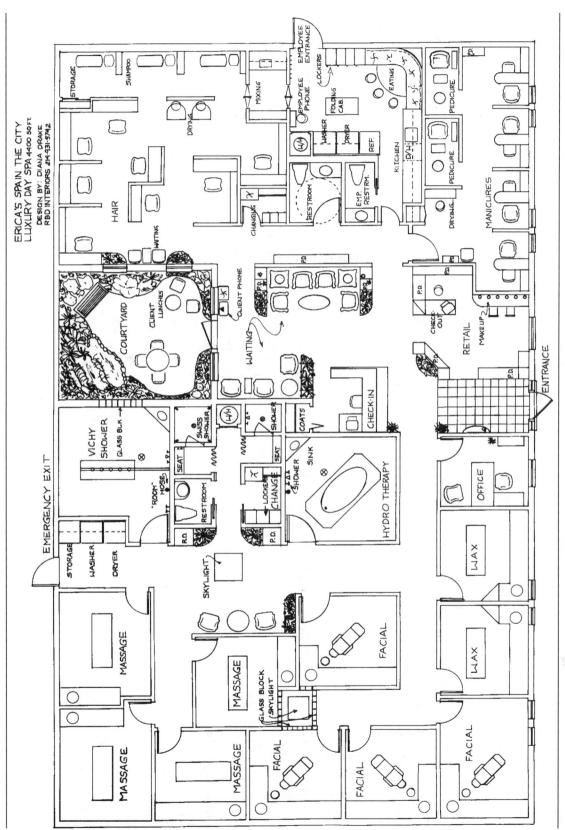

FIGURE 6-1 *Sample floor plan for luxury market day spa. (P.D. represents product display.)*

DETAILS FOR UPPER MIDDLE DAY SPA—3,100 SQUARE FOOT

Spa Includes:

Consultation table and 2 chairs

Changing room with 8 half lockers, hanging hooks, and bench with hamper below

2 Facial rooms

2 Massage rooms

2 Wax rooms

1 Vichy shower with "room" hose, walls and floor tiled

1 Hydrotherapy room with standard shower and "room" hose, walls and floor tiled

1 Swiss shower/standard shower combination with dry-off area

1 Small restroom

2 Waiting chairs

Water heater

Greenery (Mix good fake with natural—it really expands the range)

Display

Storage closet (in changing room)

Hair Includes:

5 Hair stations

2 Shampoo stations

2 Hair dryers

2 Waiting

Changing room

Storage closet

Display

Nails Includes:

2 Nail Stations

1 Pedicure room

Display cabinet

Public Areas Include:

Check-in desk with computer terminal and 42"-high client counter

Waiting for 4 with phone for client

Makeup table for 2

Check-out counter with computer terminal and display area

Display cases

Restroom with handicap facilities

Office with closet

Employee Area Includes:

1 Washer

2 Dryers

Water heater and linen storage cabinets

Kitchen—sink, dishwasher, and cabinetry

Refrigerator

Vending machine

Booth seating for 4

Phone for employees with note counter and stool

10 half lockers

Storage closet

Employee restroom

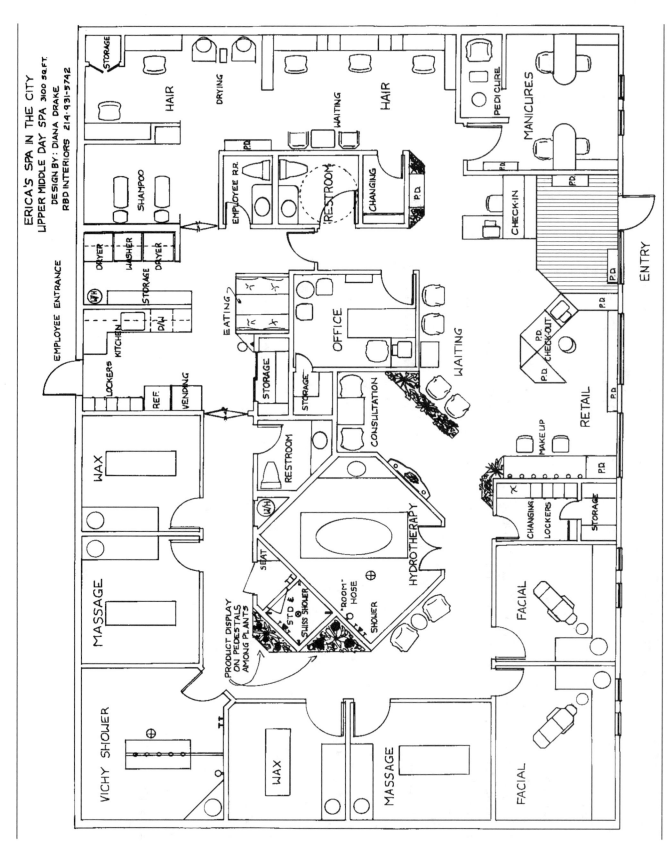

FIGURE 6-2 *Sample floor plan for upper middle market day spa. (P.D. represents product display.)*

DETAILS FOR MEDIUM DAY SPA—1,650 SQUARE FOOT

NOTE: *Design for shopping center application*

Spa Includes:

1 Changing room with 4 lockers
2 Facial rooms
1 Massage room
1 Massage or wax room
1 Vichy shower (walls and floor to be tiled and have floor drain, hand hose for hosing down room)
1 Swiss shower and standard shower combination with dry-off area
1 Small restroom
1 Display case
Storage cabinet
1 bench with hamper below

Hair Includes:

1 Changing room
2 Hair stations
1 Hair dryer
1 Shampoo
1 Waiting chair
1 Display case

Nails Includes:

2 Manicure stations
1 Pedicure (semi-private) area

Glass door and windows to "open" area up

Public Area Includes:

Check-in/check-out desk with computer and 42"-high client counter
Display cabinets—behind desk, by front door, and 4 along hallway
Makeup table
Waiting for 4
Restroom with handicap facilities
Phone for clients

Kitchen/Employee Area Includes:

1 Washer
1 Dryer
1 Water heater
Sink, refrigerator, cabinets
5 lockers for employees
Table and 4 chairs
Employee entrance
Large storage closet
Employee phone

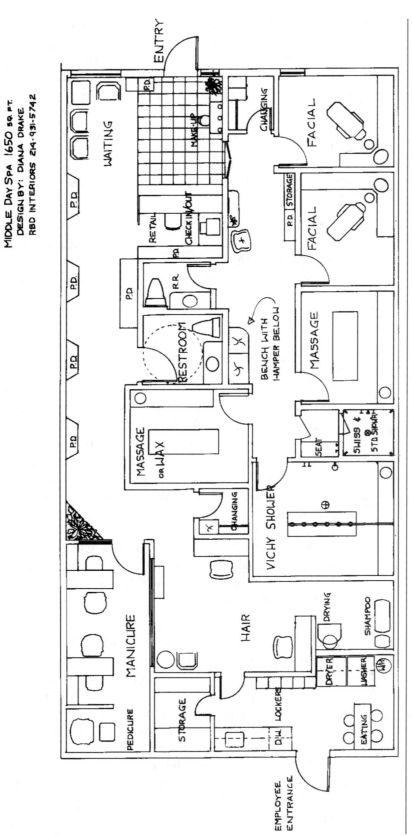

FIGURE 6-3 *Sample floor plan for middle market day spa. (P.D. represents product display.)*

So often day spa owners jump in and build without permits before investigating the requirements of the state board of cosmetology or the Department of Health, and very costly problems result later. According to the Internal Revenue Service, "Ignorance of the law is no excuse." This is also true with any other governing body and to say after it's too late, "I didn't know that," doesn't work. Before you embark on opening a day spa, you must be aware of all requirements. Although this book cannot guide you in all regulatory issues, the following may provide some assistance in common issues. You are responsible and the author takes no responsibility in any manner for business issues and regulations.

Construction

You must consider zoning, building codes and permits, labor unions, water, sewage, fire sprinklers, emergency exits, electrical requirements and limitations, and ADA (Americans with Disabilities Act) requirements. These issues are important not just for permits, but also for budgeting purposes.

Licensure

Hair, nails, and esthetics are normally governed by the state board of cosmetology. In some states the beauty and barber boards are combined, and in some states they all fall under the Department of Health or even Trades. Massage therapy and body treatments usually fall under the Department of Health if it is a licensed profession in your state. In many states, it falls under county or city codes, even including the police department's vice squad (ridiculous isn't it!). When in doubt, contact cosmetology and massage therapy schools for guidance. And then contact the licensing agency directly. Advice from a school won't protect you legally.

In most states you will have individual licenses for the technicians and a license for the facility itself. In some cases, there may be multiple facility licenses required. In addition to the day spa (salon in most states) license, you will have to adhere to state requirements for many things in the day spa. Be sure to obtain the guidelines prior to construction. For example, in the state of Texas, treatment areas shouldn't have carpeting. If you spent thousands of dollars and then had to tear it out, it would be a very costly mistake.

OSHA

The Occupational Safety and Hazard Administration (OSHA) has very strict requirements now for businesses with employees. Even though it may seem like a hassle to be compliant, it's really for your and everyone's protection. Although the regulations refer more to the handling of potentially dangerous substances, some construction issues may be pertinent. For example, if you do extractions or waxing where there is a possibility of bloodborne pathogens, you are required to have special disposal capabilities for the lancets and disposables. You may want to construct a special storage cabinet for the disposables and put the sharps container on the wall. Understanding all OSHA regulations is imperative, and ignorance can result in thousands of dollars in fines. Ventilation of chemicals in the nail and hair areas come under OSHA as well, so it's much better to know what is required in advance.

. . . .

SPA POINT

Like it or not, you are governed in this industry by a number of regulatory agencies including but not limited to state board of cosmetology, Department of Health, local zoning and permits, and OSHA. Ignorance of the requirements will not protect you from penalty for grievous mistakes, so it's better to research all the requirements in advance of construction and opening. It may save you a lot of time and money.

. . . .

Synopsis

There is probably nothing more exciting and challenging than developing your own day spa. If you care enough to do it, you must care enough to do it right. This is not a project that should be contemplated on a whim or done overnight. There are many more issues beyond choosing pretty carpets and wall coverings. The potential survival and success of your business may hinge on the decisions you make at the beginning. You must think as a businessperson and research everything extensively.

As with all things, you get what you pay for. If you want the ultimate, you will have to spend some money. If you are spending a lot of money, you should seek the advice of experts in all fields related to the project. Spending $50,000 on equipment and then trying to tile the wet room yourself after work at night may be a terrible mistake. Think carefully about where you must save money and where you must spend. If you hire consultants, designers, and architects, be absolutely certain they have experience in this field. There is a dramatic difference between designing salons and day spas and an office or a restaurant.

Review

1. Name a few important points to consider in choosing the location.

2. Is the square footage important?

3. What are a few advantages of hiring an interior designer?

4. What is the most expensive area to construct in a day spa?

5. Is it good to have the hydrotherapy tub and the Vichy shower put in the same wet room? Why?

6. About what size room is necessary for a wet room?

7. Is it important for a dry room being used for massage to have a sink?

8. What are some of the areas that are considered public areas?

9. Why is it useful to separate the check-in area from the check-out area in a large day spa?

10. Is noise a factor in placing the rooms in a day spa? Why?

11. Should the owner have an office or is it a waste of space?

12. What is a problem associated with music choices?

13. Does a day spa need a retail display area? Why?

14. What are some of the regulatory agencies involved in the day spa business?

15. Why is it important to investigate regulations and laws in advance of construction?

CHAPTER 7
Spa Story Development/Presentation _____

OVERVIEW

You'll enjoy this chapter because this is where the story begins to come together. Now let's assume that you've hired your consultants, contractors, and construction people, and they are in construction progress. If your contractors tell you it will be six weeks to completion, be sure to add on three to four weeks to that because it usually runs longer than planned and certainly longer than you want. But that's okay because you have plenty to do in the interim.

You should order your major equipment four to six weeks ahead of the date you really want it in (and perhaps longer if you're having anything custom built; custom colors for hydrotherapy tubs are sometimes available but you will need three to four months to get them from Europe). Hopefully it will come earlier and this will give you time to open everything, put it together, and practice with it before opening your doors. If there are any equipment problems, you'll have ample time to get that taken care of. If you are actually constructing a day spa and it's dirty and dusty, have your equipment shipped to your home or a friend's place. Have it somewhere you can set it up and work with it. You will have employee training prior to opening anyway, as will be covered later. So now, time to get to work on other aspects of the business.

PACKAGING THE PROJECT

This is a very important part of the business and most often left to the end, hit or miss, or entirely ignored until the spa has been open for weeks or months. You are far better off getting this all organized in the beginning.

Accounting Systems

First and foremost you need to obtain an accountant. If possible, find someone with experience in the beauty business. That makes it easier to consult and advise you on normal profit margins and costs in the industry. But this is not absolutely necessary and is frankly hard to find.

If you plan to open a large day spa with ten or more employees, it's far better to get your systems on computer. If you are working alone, then perhaps a computer is not necessary at the beginning. Of late, some wonderful software systems are available. If you decide to computerize, research it well. Don't buy the first package you see. Talk to other day spa owners in the size and scale you expect your business to be for proper comparisons. If you are opening a very large business with many employees and several product lines, computerizing is imperative. The following will cover some of the capabilities you may want the system to handle, again depending on your size.

BASIC ACCOUNTING

This includes revenue and expenses, budgets, inventory control, and financial statements including profit and loss. A monthly report should be available to you for your own internal tracking purposes. The system is only as good as the person using it. You must track your business yourself, not just count on the accountant.

INVENTORY CONTROL

You should have a system to control the movement of your products, whether by FIFO (first in first out and preferable in this business) or LIFO (last in first out). Inventory control will be discussed more fully in chapter 9, but if you can computerize it, you'll have a better ability to track what has sold, what is a slow seller, when you should reorder, and what's missing. Some software packages also offer a bar coding system that you can tie to your products and services. This has the advantage of simplifying close-out and sales. It will also help prevent mathematical errors on purchases. A bar coding system is a real time saver.

CLIENT TRACKING

If you can keep great records on your clients' service and retail habits as well as personal information, this will become your best marketing tool in the future. You must keep some records on each client on file anyway. By computerizing it and keeping it up-to-date you'll have a valuable tool. In a large operation, a computer is the optimum way to do this. It will also pull your mailing lists for promotional activities if done right. Be sure that it has the capability to produce mailing lists and labels.

PAYROLL

If you have a large staff, payroll is a weekly or bi-weekly nightmare by hand, particularly if you have variable commission rates, incentive programs, and/or promotions. Computerization in this area can save you hours and hours of headaches. If you feel you are too small for a system, there are services out there such as ADP that can help you with your payroll and federal reporting.

WORD PROCESSING

To produce your own letters, flyers, and newsletters you'll need a word processing package.

SCHEDULING

In a fast-growing or large business, scheduling on the computer will be a real blessing, particularly from the standpoint of being able to move the client through any number of services or to book other technicians for a service if the primary service giver is already booked (Figure 7-1). A word to

FIGURE 7-1 *A computer system may be one of the wisest investments you make in your business. A computer will be very helpful for scheduling, among other things.*

the wise (which will be discussed later also)—do not give your clients the impression that they can only receive a service from one technician. The client should be a client of the spa, not the technician.

If you're not extremely familiar with computers and software, your accountant and other spa owners may be able to help you in choosing the system. Research well, it's a real hassle to change software systems a year down the road. The hardware can be purchased usually at computer stores or through your software expert. The software is the most important issue in the system. Software programs may cost in the hundreds or thousands of dollars. If you find two you like and one is dramatically less expensive, it is prudent to find out why the big price difference. Cheaper is not necessarily better.

"The biggest problem I have is in communication and scheduling. Almost every problem we have deals with one or the other."—
David Miller, David & Mary's, Indianapolis

. . . .

SPA POINT

It's all well and good to invest in a computer system, but if you don't use it fully and effectively, it's a waste and down the road an issue you will truly regret. Sometimes it's easy to forget to update and input purchases, but if you will properly, it will become a magnificent marketing tool. As will be stated numerous times in this text, you cannot make your business survive and prosper by being technically great at massage. You must have a business mind as well and pay attention to the business side.

. . . .

Policies and Procedures

As much of a headache as this will seem at first, if you plan to have employees now or later, you really must have a policies and procedures manual.

This will set out the guidelines with a clear working relationship between both of you. Just as with your business plan, it will organize you and help you look practically at your business. You may still want to have a written contract with your employees, but the policies and procedures manual itself should be the rule book from which to operate. You may think you're not IBM and don't need it, but consider this: even when you're playing a board game, isn't it helpful sometimes between friends to have the rules available? Additionally, in any labor dispute, it's a sign of good planning and organization to be able to refer to the policies both you and the employee have agreed upon. If you are a one-person spa, is it necessary? Why not? It keeps you on track about what's important, and if you're successful you will have employees eventually.

The manner in which you write your manual will also set a specific tone to your employees. If written with strong commanding language, it may be a put-off to your employee. Kathy Driscoll, owner of The Spa at The Houstonian, developed a most positive yet mutually committed manual. Her philosophy is, "It must be a win win for both sides...it must clearly state what I expect and at the same time let them know all the benefits of being here."

The manual itself should be attractive, well designed, easy to read, be contained in a folder or cover of some type to encourage the employee to value it, and should contain a signature page in duplicate on which the employee acknowledges agreement with all points. The owner keeps one copy and the other signed copy is retained in the manual.

The following includes some of the subjects that should be covered in the manual.

STATEMENT OF BENEFITS

This is a terrific section. List the benefits of working in your day spa. List the obvious ones like vacation pay, sick leave, insurance, and bonuses and also the prestige, education in new equipment and services, ability to get to meet famous people (if applicable or important), and special programs. Include anything that sets your business on the cutting edge. Some of the benefits may not even seem like a benefit to you, but if it is a plus, list it. It can be quite an impressive list and really enhances the employment package. It also starts the manual off on a really positive note.

EXPECTATIONS/JOB DESCRIPTION

We all do better in any work situation if we know clearly what's expected. In most instances in this industry, there is always a lack of time to properly initiate and train a new employee, particularly in view of the turnover in the business. As such, you may forget to properly inform the employee of what you expect. The job description should clearly outline the duties, dress code, attitudes, client relations, compensation, hygiene and sanitary procedures, and evaluation procedure. A good safety net for you is to include one statement at the end of the description of duties, such as "and miscellaneous duties as required." This will cover you for anything you may have forgotten or new duties you want to add.

SPA RULES

This will include policies for the entire operation—days off/hours/shifts, set-up and clean-up, parking, use of inventory, absences, laundry duties, lunch and break times (time and where to eat, and what not to cook, such as popcorn the odor from which spreads throughout the spa), opening and closing, telephone procedures, and various team duties.

PERIODIC EVALUATION FORM

Include a sample of your evaluation form or procedure. It's advisable to evaluate the progress of your employees once or twice a year to keep them on track, improve on weak areas, and praise them for accomplishments. The form should include such subjects as performance, productivity, client relations and retention, attitude, level of cooperation, and eagerness to grow and learn. It's not a bad idea to have a form for the employees to evaluate the business as well. This keeps them part of the team and allows them the opportunity for viable input. The spa evaluation form might include areas of strength and weakness, things that might be changed or added, policies that might make the business run more smoothly, and overall feelings. In both evaluation forms, the goal should not be to criticize without options for improvement. They should be positive and improvement oriented, not negative.

"It's difficult to correct an employee, they always take it personally and resent the correction. It's difficult to control the way they dress, how they handle clients, and it's so easy for them to just ignore issues."—Leah Kovitz, New Image by Leah, Tucson, Arizona

. . . .

SPA POINT

The policies and procedures manual is a vital part of running a well-organized business and can be a great growing tool for both the employer and employee if done well. The owner should re-evaluate the manual from time to time and adjust it according to current needs. Do not expect it to cover every issue that will ever occur; it's impossible unless you want a very down, oppressive book. Keep it to the point and upbeat. And finally, be sure to use it with every employee, not just at the first launch with the first group.

. . . .

Employment Issues

This is always the most important and most difficult part of running a business, but at the same time, it's also the best part of the business if you approach it right. Perhaps the real key to making it work is to remember Kathy Driscoll's statement, "It has to be a win win for both sides or it doesn't work." In any business there's always the "them against us" issue. Another factor that is amusing to all owners is that the average employee tends to feel that the owner is rich or wouldn't have a business. The reality is that most owners are not rich. If the owner was really all that rich, would she be there? It's not to say that you can't get rich in this industry, but rich is a subjective issue anyway. What's rich to one person may not be to another. And "monetarily rich" may not be the main goal either. The important consideration here is not "them against us" or "rich." It should be that "we're a team working together for the same goal." All roles are equally important.

All working together in harmony make a really successful business. Now let's look at the major aspects of personnel issues.

NOTE: *With the exception of the information about independent contractor status, all other references will assume employer/employee status.*

EMPLOYEE VERSUS INDEPENDENT CONTRACTOR

This is probably one of the most controversial issues in the beauty industry. It is the strong belief of this author that in most cases, employee status works more successfully in the long run than independent contractor status. However, there are some situations for the esthetician or massage therapist where independent contractor status is better. This would be where a salon basically has little interest in the esthetics department and would rather rent out the space and be done with it. Some hairdressing salon owners don't understand esthetics or have had bad experiences and prefer to lease the space to a person specializing in the field. This is common. However, the concern of this book is the full day spa, with an obvious large concentration on total body care. So for the most part, a day spa would not come under this category.

Beyond this, it's important for you to contact the Internal Revenue Service and your insurance company to clearly know the characteristics and problems that could arise from independent contractor status. This abbreviated list will give you a brief idea of how the IRS views the differences between the two.

EMPLOYEE	INDEPENDENT CONTRACTOR
The spa controls the appointment bookings.	The individual does all personal bookings.
Services are performed exclusively for one business.	Services may be provided for multiple entities.
The spa provides the work place.	The individual provides own work place.
The spa owns and operates the telephones.	The individual has personal telephone.
The spa sets the work schedule.	The individual determines own work schedule.
The spa provides fringe benefits.	The spa provides no fringe benefits.
The spa pays an hourly wage.	The individual receives payments.
There is an ongoing business relationship.	The relationship with spa terminates at specified point.
The spa provides the tools and products.	The individual pays own expenses, purchases own products.
The employee has minimal or restricted powers.	The individual provides tools and products.
The work is controlled and/or directed by the spa owner.	Work is not supervised or controlled by the spa.

The IRS has specific guidelines available. Contact your local or state IRS office for further information.

And finally, one of the most important points from a spa owner management standpoint that must be considered is, if you plan to adhere to IRS regulations, you must realize that you have no control over that individual. Is that what you want? If you decide you want everyone wearing black and white, what does that mean? If you want a "well-greased" team, then contract labor is not for you. Keep in mind, in simple terms, when you lease to independent contractors you are no longer their employer, you're really only their landlord, and as such you're then in the property business, not the spa business.

. . . .

SPA POINT

The Internal Revenue Service is very strict about independent contractor status versus employee status. If you want to be a landlord and rent space, that's fine, but if you want to control the activities and management of your spa, you must operate with employees. If you want a team and want to control the appointments, product lines, and policies you must operate with employee status. Contact the IRS for complete information, including fines and penalties.

. . . .

HIRING EMPLOYEES

Do you want to hire an experienced technician or a person right out of school whom you'll have to train? This is a choice you will make and may change from time to time. The advantage to hiring someone right out of school is the ability to train the person as you want. The experienced person, on the other hand, may be a little more recalcitrant about learning your techniques. If, however, you have no experience yourself and plan to be the business owner, not technician, you should look for an experienced technician.

Hiring young or old, male or female are questions you should decide on your own. The best route is to hire based upon the personality and qualifications of the applicant. You have also to observe the labor laws related to hiring. As is commonly known, this industry tends to have a very high employee turnover rate. It's too bad but it's a fact. Therefore, in the hiring there should be considerations on both owner's side and the employee's side.

Do not advertise for a technician with a clientele. This can be problematical. In the first place, an ad stating this really means you're trying to hire a clientele, not necessarily a highly qualified individual. It puts the emphasis on the clientele, not the expertise of the technician. In addition, down the road when that employee chooses to leave you, do you really want him/her to feel comfortable taking clients? No, of course not. Don't worry, the technician will anyway, but at least from the beginning you are not endorsing the concept of bringing or taking clientele. If you hire someone with experience and you feel that he/she is highly qualified to work for you, the clientele that will come with the employee will come or not anyway. And then on the back side, when the employee leaves you, there is a clear understanding that the clients of the spa are in reality and in honesty clients of the spa.

Job Interviews

It has been suggested in management books that in any hiring situation, there should be at least two if not three interviews. The first time everyone is nervous and on guard. The second time, each party begins to relax and get to know each other better, and by the third time, the guards are down and the real people come through. Good idea! Also, it's important for both the employer and prospective employee to interview the other party. This should never be a one-sided issue. Both sides must work well together, and if it works only for the spa, the employee won't last, and if the employee goes to work in the wrong market then time is wasted for a major market change. In other words, if the employee eventually wants to open a day spa, it does no good to work in a mass market operation if the ultimate goal is upper middle or luxury market. The client won't follow. From the owner standpoint, it's a very costly proposition to hire, train, and develop an employee. To hire too easily is to waste time and energy. It might be well to think of the employer/employee relationship as similar to marriage in hopes and planning for a long-term relationship.

"Turnover will be your biggest issue. Develop programs that keep staff interested and challenged, and wanting to stay for the next 'event.' Money is important, but so is personal growth."— Marguerite Rivel, Spa Director, The Broadmoor, Colorado Springs

Employment Contracts

Employment contracts are designed to clearly delineate the agreements between both parties. In many cases, the employment contract is devised to lock the employee in because of the time, education, and costs related to developing that employee. That's fine, but be realistic. If you state that the technician after termination can't work anywhere within a one-hundred-mile radius for ten years it obviously won't hold up in court. You cannot deprive an individual of being able to make a living. But if you have a reimbursement clause for educational expenses if the employee leaves before a specified period, that's fair. If you choose to have employee contracts, which is not always the case, you should check with your attorney for the legalities and language for your own contracts. Contracts are effective only if good for both parties, so don't attempt to hang the prospective employee out to dry.

Who To Hire

This is rather subjective and ultimately you will know. But in simple terms you want to hire people who are caring, eager, excited about your business, have a nurturing personality, are potentially trained in more than one specialty, and can retail products. This industry is not historically strong in retailing, rather more adept at the technical skills. This can be a disadvantage to you because retail is where the big profits are for both you and the employee. Look for good selling skills or at least an open mind to learn and value retail (Figure 7-2). Look for the type of personality and characteristics that blend in well with your spa and philosophies. You wouldn't want an extremely eclectic, liberal individual if you and your spa concepts are staunchly conservative.

FIGURE 7-2 *Hire employees who are skilled in their particular field and who are (or have the potential to be) excellent retail sales people.*

A quick comment about hiring your front desk (receptionist) person. This is the most important person on staff, and is traditionally the least paid. It's a mistake. This is the person who has the strongest initial impact on the client, whether on the telephone or when the client comes in. This person needs to have a great telephone voice, be bubbly and personable, patient and able to handle a number of things at once, and caring of both the clientele and employees. This should not be your least paid person. Take good care of this person; he/she can make or break your business.

EMPLOYEE COMPENSATION

There are many methods and styles of payment plans. Some spas pay per hour; some are strictly commission. This industry is normally a commission-based system but often with variations. For example, a typical straight commission system might be based on 50 percent for services and 10 percent on retail products. This is about the national average. However, the savvy business owner should develop an incentive system with small percentage increases on larger volume. If your normal markup on products is 100 percent (or double), a rule of thumb would be to never go above 20 percent, and that would be on quite a large volume of retail. Between 10 percent and 15 percent is quite easy for an owner to develop incentives.

Some spas will start a new employee with guarantee or draw for a specified amount of time in order for the employee to survive while building business. This length of time varies but should be limited by mutual agreement. A guarantee means that no matter what, the employee is guaranteed a certain sum per week (don't make it too high for fear of killing incentive). A draw means that a minimum guarantee is established, but when the employee exceeds it, he/she goes on straight commission. Some even make the draw retroactive, where the employee is liable later to repay draw money when the sum wasn't reached. This is not advisable; it creates ill will quickly.

A suggestion for the employee: if you believe you're an excellent retailer and the spa owner isn't too eager to provide extra percentages on higher volume, you may want to negotiate a little lower percentage on service and increase the retail, for example, 45 percent on service and 15 percent on retail. This is certainly to your advantage, but it's also to the good of the owner. Some spa owners are even more creative and establish an educational budget where a small percentage of the employee's retail percentage is put in a fund and matched by the owner. Then when a viable educational event is chosen, there is money available. Periodically, the spa may even want to offer bonuses or extra percentages on specific promotions.

Even though 50 percent on service and 10 percent on product are nationally the most common, there are no hard and fast rules. If you are the owner of an extremely famous and prestigious spa and just the mere experience of working there guarantees prestige for the employee next time, your percentages may be lower and still work well. Be as creative as you can keep up with accounting-wise. Be fair, and remember to create something that will benefit both you and the employee.

Fringe Benefits

Fortunately this industry is evolving more and more into a "company" concept. With this is a dramatic improvement in fringe benefit packages. It will not be what large corporations or the federal government can provide, but it will be a very important bonding tool for the spa owner if you offer benefits. You may need to have the employee pay for or participate in the costs for health insurance, but it's a very important benefit because of the tremendous health care costs. It certainly shows you care. As for vacations, sick pay, bonuses, and profit-sharing plans, do what you can as you grow. You most likely can't offer everything at the beginning, but keep it in mind for future goals. Little bonuses now and again are people winners. Usually with an employee it isn't the dollar amount of the bonus, it's the fact that you care. Sometimes just a card goes a long way.

A fringe benefit is not, however, lending your employees money. This can open a huge bucket of worms. Have a no-lending policy included in your employee manual. Then in a real emergency, you may choose to make an exception to the rule, but it's dangerous.

EDUCATION

There's no question that the technology in this industry changes at a very fast pace. You must keep your employees up-to-date. It's your responsibility and also the employee's (Figure 7-3). Staying on top of your industry is a professional duty. The question is, who pays for it? There are as many ways to handle advanced educational issues as there are compensation plans. Whatever you decide, you must be sure that the employee understands clearly at the hiring stage. Normally, all product knowledge and spa-related education is the responsibility of the spa owner. Technical updates are nor-

FIGURE 7-3 *State-of-the-art skills and continuing education are the keys to your staff's success.*

mally the responsibility of the technician. However, it's wise to work together on a game plan. It's very important to cross-train your technicians in as many departments as possible. The more versatile the employee the more valuable he/she becomes. Education through seminars, lectures, and attending shows can be considered perks, bonuses, and incentives. You have to keep your employees motivated and prevent burnout. Education is probably the best way to do this.

If you send your employee somewhere for education and it's costly, particularly in the beginning, you may want to have a written agreement for reimbursement if the employee leaves for any reason prior to an agreed-upon time. Many an owner has spent thousands of dollars in education only to have the employee leave a few weeks or months later. In fairness, the employee shouldn't allow the owner to spend a lot of money if the intent is to leave soon. Education is such a key part of the ongoing success of a business that both owner and employee must be willing to continually update and grow.

TERMINATION

Termination is a sticky issue. The employer must follow labor laws (contact your local labor board for guidance) and be clear about any and all reasons for termination. Warnings prior to termination must be documented in writing. The larger issue, however, is the termination on the part of the employee. Since, as has been stated, turnover is high, many employees do what I might call "the midnight skip," that is, quitting without notice or professional actions. The reality of a walkout is damage to both sides. The employee may be upset and be excited to "stick it to the employer," but the reality is that if the client is hurt the employee will suffer as well somehow. If, as an employee, you decide to resign, do it professionally. Don't skip out; don't "steal" the clientele; don't talk bad to your clients about the spa owner. And spa owner, if the employee resigns properly, you may still want him/her to leave right away (usually the best way for both sides), but treat the person with respect. If you know where the employee has gone, offer that information if a client asks. The client will find the technician anyway, and it only makes you look bad to hide that information. Both sides must act professionally. The interesting part of this business is the fact that you will certainly cross paths again somehow, so be cautious in burning those bridges.

"It's very difficult trying to handle the business side if you're doing the service side as well. My preference now is to build my business to the point where I can pass it on to my staff but still maintain a select clientele of my own. Plus it's important to keep my own hands on the pulse of changes, etc. in the industry."—
Lynn Kirkpatrick, With Class, A Day Spa, Tyler, Texas

. . . .

SPA POINT

There are few hard and fast rules about hiring and handling employees. Whether you are the owner or employee, it won't always be perfect. From the owner's standpoint, you will want to expect perfect devotion, twenty-four-hour-a-day caring, and perfection. This is impossible. Remember that if the employee could do everything perfectly in your eyes, he or she would probably be an owner, not your employee. And employee, you have a great mandate too: to give devotion, loyalty, and the best job possible for that spa while you're there. You may aspire to own a spa someday too, and that's fine. Treat your owner with professional respect now. The bottom line for both owner and employee, you must work together and be accountable and responsible to make it work. It must work well for both sides or it won't work. It's that simple.

. . . .

Developing the Character of the Day Spa

As the title would suggest, the character of the day spa is who and what the spa represents. It begins with the name of the day spa and continues with the literature, pricing, menus, and the like. This is one of the really fun parts of getting your spa together. But it's also very important. The determinations you make at the beginning may be hard to change later.

NAMING

This may seem simple, but it should take a lot of thought. The name will represent you everywhere, from filling out your tax forms to the telephone book listing, from your sign to the brochure, and on and on. The name is who you are. Your name should reflect what impression you want clients to receive. If you are a full service day spa with face, body, hair, and nails, would "The Face Place" be a good name? Absolutely not. It limits your impression out there to facial services. How about a hair salon with the name "Whackers?" Want to get your hair cut there?

Just as you don't want to limit yourself by the name, you don't want to date yourself by your name. The name should also reflect the market with which you want to identify. If you plan to cater to the luxury market, would you name your $200,000 day spa "Susie's Beauty Box?" Consider the image, spelling, and design of your name carefully. Make sure it looks good in literature as well as on a sign and that it's a name your clients can pronounce. If they can't pronounce it, they can't pass it on to friends. Also, in the naming, you may or may not want to develop a logo or use you own name. A favorite of mine is David & Mary, Indianapolis (Figure 7-4). It's simple but elegant and represents the two great personalities who determined to build a day spa and make it a prominent entity in Indianapolis, and they did. Their name value alone in that city has turned out to be phenomenal. The look is classy but simple and certainly doesn't limit them in any way. For that matter, they could use the name and open a restaurant, boutique, pet grooming center, or anything. They have no limitations whatsoever.

FIGURE 7-4 *Business card from David & Mary.*

Body Treatments

With Class A DAY SPA has the most sophisticated and individualized equipment and treatments available in the country to insure your way to a new invigorated body.

Body treatments for the 90's are an absolute must in today's stress related society.

Hydrotherapy includes the use of water pressure via the specialized Hydrotherapy Tub, Vichy Shower, and Swiss Shower to invigorate, revitalize and relieve stress.

Treatments concentrate on the use of plants, aromatherapy and minerals derived from the sea to revitalize, tone and condition the body. Certain treatments cater to specialized needs such as cellulite or muscle tension.

Relax, enjoy and join us for any or a combination of the following offerings.

ANTI-CELLULITE TREATMENT

A highly effective treatment for help in the prevention or reduction of cellulite. An application of stimulating formula followed by a warm pack of seaweed enriched with essential oils increases ones natural metabolical functions to help eliminate cellulite over time _____ $45.00

FIRMING BUST TREATMENT

A good skin care program must not be reserved just for the care of the face. The bust and neckline, more than other parts of the body, are extremely susceptible to aging. A carefully delicate and modest treatment designed to recondition, tone and tighten the sensitive bust area _____ $45.00

STRESS RELIEF TREATMENT

This calming and soothing treatment is specifically designed to relieve the stiffness and soreness due to tension or sports related fatigue. The deep penetration plus warming effect is surpassed only by the purifying effects of essential oils which are gently massaged in the area of discomfort _____ $45.00

FULL BODY SALT GLOW

An invigorating full body massage using 100% natural dead sea salts combined with an emulsion to remove dead skin cells and increase circulation to dull dry skin. This treatment finishes with a special skin conditioner leaving the skin soft and smooth with a healthy glow _____ $45.00

SEA MUD FULL BODY MASK

A concise formula of seaweed, vegetable extracts and essential oils are combined to produce a mud rich in minerals and trace elements to help restore tissue elasticity and soften the skin _____ $65.00
(Includes Vichy or Swiss Shower)

FULL BODY ALGAE TREATMENT

The special properties of seaweed are specifically blended to nourish, hydrate and purify the body. This combination along with essential oils of Birch, Juniper and Cypress stimulate the metabolism, leaving the skin firm and refined, thus providing a healthy glow _____ $70.00

HYDROTHERAPY TUB & UNDERWATER TREATMENT

Your own private tub treatment with customized underwater air targeting your specific needs. Hydrotherapy, by far the most up-to-date and comprehensive body treatment concept _____ $65.00

FIGURE 7-5 *Do the descriptions of your treatments inspire clients to want an appointment* now? *(Menu from With Class A Day Spa.)*

FIGURE 7-6 *Consider the menu for The Spa at the Broadmoor. Descriptions are concise, allowing room to list several treatments.*

DEVELOPING THE MENU OF SERVICES AND BROCHURE/BUSINESS CARDS

Please refer to chapter 8 for more detailed information on this. In the chapter on purchasing it was briefly mentioned that you must budget for brochures, price lists, and the like. Just as with the name, the brochure you create to explain your services is a vital piece of the puzzle. The brochure represents you out there in the world where you can't be. If the spa is elegant and your brochure is just a hand-typed list of services copied on neon paper the impression given to the potential client is incongruous. On the other hand, if your literature is superb, the impression will be that as well. During your research and spa visitations, you should obtain samples of different brochures to give you ideas. Don't think if you're small that you don't need a nice brochure. You may soon discover that your brochure is so great that it quickly helps build you into something bigger. The brochure itself should be a piece that the client wants to keep, not throw in the trash on the way out the door.

Your menu of services should be listed and explained to the extent that the client understands what you have to offer and is inspired to a visit (Figure 7-5). Some spas offer an extensive list of different services, and some prefer to keep it rather simple (Figure 7-6). This is a personal preference issue. Sometimes if you list fifteen different versions of a facial, it can put off clients. How do they know what to choose? On the other hand, if you have an unusual treatment or one that has a specific name provided by your product supplier, the name may be important. If that treatment name has national or international recognition, it's advisable to list it specifically. As you develop your menu, it might be wise to have some of your nonprofessional friends or family look it over and give you their impressions. The brochure is for the layperson, so that person's view is valuable.

The business cards should follow suit and match the mood and ambiance of the spa. All employees should have and use their business cards. You may have to teach your employees how to use them. Business cards should be carried at all times and given out to any person who might become a client. The business card should be attractive and attention-getting. Just as with the brochure, if it's unusual and attractive, the client will want to keep it.

FIGURE 7-7 *This piece describes both full- and half-day packages.*

Other Personal Care

Foot or Hand Massage During Facial	$15.00
Make-up Application	$30.00
Make-up Lesson - 1 hour	$45.00
Specialized Make-up (Weddings, etc.)	$75.00

Ask for special quotes for on-location make-up services

Spa Packages

Welcome ... Treat yourself to exquisite face and body treatments by our highly trained staff.

Enjoy the most luxurious spa environment available. A Day Spa provides services and treatments that are offered by the world's great spas. Spend the hour ... spend the day!

THE ULTIMATE — The ultimate in a getaway frame of mind. Hydrotherapy with underwater treatment, a full body mask, a spa pedicure, a manicure with paraffin, an individualized facial, catered lunch, and a full body Swedish massage
(Approx. 7 hrs.) _____ $250.00 (Value $285)

THE ESCAPE — Disappear in the world of total relaxation. Swedish massage, deep pore cleansing facial, lunch, pedicure and manicure with pariffin (Approx. 4 hrs.) _____ $120.00 (Value $145)

EXECUTIVE GETAWAY — Regain your sanity with a getaway for the ever busy executive. Hydrotherapy tub and Swedish massage
(Approx. 2½ hrs.) _____ $95.00 (Value $110)

PAMPER ME — Just relax and let us pamper you as you have always wanted to be. Individualized facial, manicure and pedicure
(Approx. 2½ hrs.) _____ $70 (Value $80)

BEST FACE FORWARD — Let our make-up experts show you how to contour, highlight and enhance your best features. Makeup and makeup lesson (Approx. 1 hr.) _____ $60.00 (Value $75)

OR / A LA CARTE! — Let us create one of our custom designed days for a wonderful gift or just for you — include flowers, limousine ... limited only by your imagination.

be treated with Class at . . .

A DAY SPA

621 B Chase Drive
Tyler, Texas 75701

903/581-1745
By Appointment

FIGURE 7-8 *The name you give your packages should exemplify the goal of the treatments.*

PACKAGES AND SERIES

Since the day spa really evolved from the resort/destination spa, the idea of packages is more or less integrally part of the day spa concept. The idea that someone can visit your day spa for one service, one-half day, or one full day makes the package concept ideal (Figure 7-7). You will want to develop a number of packages—full day, half day, men's, bridal, teenage, luxurious, business. As you begin to make your combinations, consider the goal of that package and how it will be described. Then offer the services that coincide (Figure 7-8).

Another way to make a package is to include some popular services that sell easily and then include a service that may be unknown or different into the package. For example, men readily have massages and manicures. So make a package including a body massage, manicure, and hydrotherapy tub treatment. And be sure to give all male-oriented packages male names, such as A Gentleman's Hand Treatment or Sports Facial. The hydrotherapy tub treatment may be new to him, but he'll purchase it because he wants the manicure and massage. Then if he likes it, he now knows about hydrotherapy.

Selling a treatment series is another form of a package. If you want the client to purchase a package of three, six, or twelve weekly facial treatments, you may want to offer a 5–10 percent discount on the package, depending on its total value. The advantage for both you and the client is the ability to obtain a commitment to good skin care (Figure 7-9). It makes the client commit to coming every week and it makes you commit to promised results by close repetitive visits. Discounting the series is common, but another way to

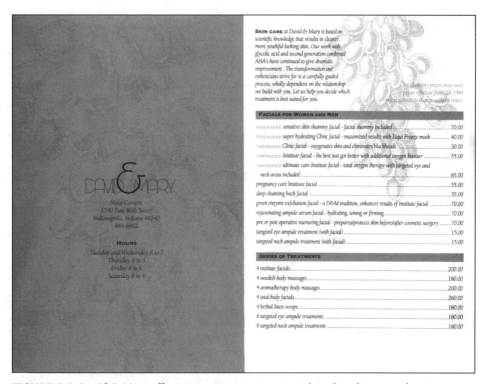

FIGURE 7-9 *David & Mary offer treatments in a series, as explained in this menu of services.*

do this is to offer no dollar discount but to include a home care product with the series as a gift. The advantage to this system is to get the product in the client's hand. Giving a gift with the purchase of a service or other product is called a GWP, gift with purchase, and is very common in the retail marketplace, along with PWPs, which are purchase with purchase items (i.e., a lesser priced item when a full priced item is bought or a specific amount is spent). The treatment value of the program is enhanced, the client doesn't have to buy that product, and you have given a product with a certain retail value that only cost you half (if 100 percent markup). Everyone wins in this scenario.

The catch to series selling is to make clearcut expiration dates. If, for example, you sell a six-week series and it takes the client a year to use it up, it wasn't really a series and you gave a discount for lesser results. If your treatments are designed to show marked improvement over that six-week period of time, the client loses the benefit of the marked improvement, and your credibility may suffer. Now obviously you won't hang the client if a week is missed, but it should be clear that it must be used in a timely fashion. Provide a tight expiration period such as eight or nine weeks and then determine how you will honor it on a case by case basis. It's important to call and remind the client a day or two before the next scheduled visit.

PRE & POST BOOT CAMP & HIGH TECH GLYCOLACTIC SKIN PEELING

Glycolactic AHA's - combined acids for safer peeling, less irritation, and more hydration

PREMIERE *super hydrating glycolactic AHA peeling*

glycolactic 15	50.00
glycolactic 30	60.00

PREMIERE *pre Boot Camp glycolactic AHA peeling, helps determine if*
other peeling is needed, 2 treatments ... 110.00

PREMIERE *post Boot Camp glycolactic AHA peeling, helps continue results*
from Boot Camp or other peels, 2 treatments ... 110.00

BOOT CAMP & HIGH TECH GLYCOLIC SKIN PEELING

Glycolic - ultimate wake-up call for skin

Clinic Boot Camp series, 4 treatments	162.50
Institute Clinic Boot Camp series, 3 treatments	225.00
glycolic 10 (with facial)	10.00
glycolic 10 / green enzyme (with facial)	25.00
glycolic 15 (with facial)	30.00
glycolic 20 (with facial)	35.00
glycolic 30 (after Boot Camp)	65.00

AHA BODY EXFOLIATION

full arms, including hands	60.00	series of six treatments	300.00
chest	60.00	series of six treatments	300.00
back	75.00	series of six treatments	390.00

BODY TREATMENTS

swedish body massage	50.00
aromatherapy body massage	55.00
parisian body polishing	75.00
wet body exfoliation	40.00
herbal paraffin body treatment	70.00
total body facial	70.00
herbal linen wrap	50.00
thalassohydrotherapy tub treatment	35.00

FIGURE 7-10 *There are many factors to consider when determining your pricing structure. Take a look at your competitors' prices, among other variables.*

PRICING THE SERVICES

This can be a difficult part of the spa development (Figure 7-10). There are some basic, logical rules. Determine your cost of treatment (labor, overhead, product usage per treatment), determine what your comfortable net profit would be on various pricing, and then set the price by subtracting all the costs from the designated price for the service. A normal net profit after all costs in this industry is between 7 and 15 percent. However, just determining this may or may not work. There are other factors that must be considered such as your competitions' prices, what your client base is willing to pay, the value of your time (professional experience) on that service, uniqueness of the treatment or product. You must be realistic and not gouge the client if you want to build.

On the other hand, if you have a very upscale salon with an expensive European line, you don't want to underprice yourself either. In some instances if it's too cheap it has no value. You may even choose to develop your menu with some higher- and lower-priced services. Some spas carry two product lines specifically for that reason, the upscale higher priced line for the luxury group and economical products for the middle group.

Raising prices is another difficult issue. Don't set your initial prices with the idea of raising them too quickly or too much as it's hard to come down. If you feel you need to increase your profits and your operating expenses have gone up 10 percent, don't increase by 10 percent. This only meets the increased expenses but doesn't add a margin for the additional profit. Price increases should not be enacted too often; it's irritating to the clients. An average of about eighteen months is probably the industry norm. It's also better not to raise prices on services and products at the same time. There's an interesting phenomenon you may experience down the road in your business. If you find that your profits are down but you're booked solid, it may be an indication of a stagnant clientele. As strange as it may sound, a substantial price increase on service may weed out some clients. This is sometimes good in order to obtain new clients that are more eager to purchase more services and products.

SALON HOURS AND APPOINTMENTS

You will certainly want to investigate the normal operation hours of your competition. In today's society, having the spa open six, even seven, days a week well into the evening and very early in the morning is prevalent. As you cringe while reading this, consider the simple fact that the day spa's major client base is the career professional. This person works hard and may want your services, but if they're available only during the same hours he/she works you lose potential business. Think of the reason why convenience stores are so effective.

If you are a small spa working alone, you may want to schedule your working hours on a fluctuating schedule according to different days of the week. Or, if you have employees and the capability, shifts may work well for you, for example, one shift from 6:00 AM to 2:00 PM and the second shift from 2:00 PM to 10:00 PM (if you want to be open that late). How about Sunday afternoons after church? You may want some part-time people to work Sunday, other staff off days, and some evenings. The majority of spa business today for a working person must be before or after the normal 9:00–5:00 hours. If, however, you're catering to the nonworking woman then regular hours might be fine.

Now, appointment issues, and this is extremely important. When appointments are made, your technician or receptionist should always call a day or two before to remind the client of the appointment. If you have established a twenty-four-hour cancellation policy and the client doesn't show up, you have the option of billing the client for the appointment or making the exception and forgiving it with no charge. It's good client relations to be rather kind on this policy until it's abused. At the point where the client is consistently late or doesn't show up, and if this negatively impacts your other clients and employees, it may be time to terminate the business relationship with this client. A bad client is not good for your business.

If you feel the necessity to ask a client not to come back, be polite but firm. If appropriate, offer the names of other businesses as suggestions to take care of the client. Be very cautious in terminating clients. Don't do it just because the client is somewhat irritating. You must remember basically that the client is always right and the mild irritation is just part of the business. But if it gets out of hand and is detrimental to other valuable clients, it's time to end the relationship. If a client just comes late, you will have to use your judgment about treating the client or rescheduling. You cannot allow a client to throw you off schedule for all the other clients. In most day spa treatments, after about 15–20 minutes it's difficult to take the client and finish the service in time without sacrificing the quality of the service. It may be better to offer the client an alternative service in the time left and rebook the original service as soon as possible.

. . . .

SPA POINT

The determinations you make as far as literature, pricing, menus, hours, and the like for your day spa really set the tone for how your business will evolve. Quality and care are a must. The name of your day spa along with the literature you develop are your ongoing spokesperson. Your menu, packages, series, and prices tell the client who and what you are. Even your hours and appointment policies speak strongly for how much you care about the client. No one part alone is a panacea. The combination brings all the basic business elements together in a form and fashion that will really go a long way in determining your market direction.

. . . .

THE LAUNCH OF YOUR DAY SPA

The moment you've planned for and anticipated for a long time is the launch of your day spa. This should be a happy, exciting time but is most often the epitome of stress and fatigue. The launch to your public is new and exciting, but for you it's been weeks, months, or even years of waiting, working, planning, and spending. Therefore don't stress yourself out more by making a big opening affair on the first day you open the door. It is strongly suggested that after the construction is done and everything has been moved in and people are hired that you merely do what is called a "soft opening," begin and promote the services to friends and neighbors. In other words, get your feet wet, work out the bugs, practice treatments and policies with your staff for a few weeks. Then and only then, after you feel comfortable with everything and after you've had a few good nights' sleeps, do your official launch.

The official launch should be well planned. Have the chamber of commerce scheduled to come out for a ribbon cutting ceremony. Plan it with an open house party. Send out press releases (see chapter 8) to all the media in the city or area (all TV and radio stations, newspapers, magazines, and the like). Make sure the opening party is congruous with the market scale to which you're wanting to cater. If, for example, you want the middle market would it be wise to have an evening gown and tails, stretch limos, "Academy Awards" affair? Perhaps not, but that might be perfect for the high middle or luxury market. Just be sure that in advance of whatever level of affair you plan, you have invitations sent out, press releases in the hands of the media, and all the staff pumped and ready to present the spa. In Chapter 8 we will discuss other media events beyond the opening, but the opening should be very important.

Be sure the spa looks immaculate and that all staff is well trained on how to tour visitors through all departments, no matter what their personal department is. You never want one technician telling a client that he/she knows nothing about another area. Your team must be selling for each other always, but particularly during the opening. Brochures and business cards must be ready and placed throughout the spa during the event. If you are able, obtain samples and literature from your suppliers and invite the supplier to send a representative to be on hand, whether at their expense or yours. It's valuable. It's nice to have a bag of literature and samples to give each visitor. Usually attendance, samples, and the like must be arranged well in advance with your suppliers.

Be sure to have a photographer on the premises to take lots of pictures of people. Then after the event you will send another press release with photos. Often the opening itself will be covered again in the society pages, but if not, having photos of clients will be valuable for your scrapbook and to give the photos to the client. After the launch, don't sit back on your laurels. Your marketing and promotion have only just begun.

· ·

SPA POINT

Your opening launch is a vital marketing effort so do it right. Open your day spa carefully and work all the bugs out before having a big open house. Then, once the system is refined, have a great opening celebration to inaugurate the launch. Immediately following be prepared for ongoing marketing efforts.

· ·

Synopsis

There are so many vital details to consider in opening a business of this nature. It may seem daunting at first, but if you make yourself a notebook and work on all the phases a little at a time you should find the experience enjoyable. Is it possible to say that hiring is the most important thing in the development? Or is it the brochure? It's really all of it. It is a business and it's all business. You have a wonderful opportunity to develop an incredibly successful venture. From the first step of considering the accounting package to the final day when you turn the key to walk into a working day spa, details are important and no one is more important than another. Sincerity and mutual benefit should be the bywords of the employment challenge, pricing and menus of services should reflect your real treatment goals, and the literature should all be a proud representation of who you plan to be in this venture. And if at all possible, do what David Miller, co-owner of David & Mary, Indianapolis, suggests: "Enjoy the journey, not just the destination!"

Review

1. When should equipment be ordered for the day spa?
2. What are a few advantages to having a computer system for the day spa?
3. Must you have a policies and procedures manual? If so why?
4. What is the benefit of an employee evaluation?
5. What is the most important reason for having employees as opposed to independent contractors?
6. Why should you not advertise for a technician with a clientele?
7. Is it important to cross-train employees?
8. Is the front desk person (receptionist) important? Why?
9. What story should the name of the salon suggest?
10. Why do packages do well in a day spa?
11. What are some of the factors to consider in determining your pricing?
12. What is an appointment cancellation policy?
13. What are possible hours that business and career clients need to be able to utilize the services of a day spa?
14. Is it possible to have shifts in a spa?
15. When should the official opening ceremony/celebration take place?

CHAPTER 8
Marketing and Retailing ————————————————

OVERVIEW

Your day spa is open and operating (Figure 8-1). Your staff is on board and functioning. Does it mean that you can rest now? In the last chapter, you had a lot of creative opportunities to develop your name, menu, and programs. Now, however, is the time to really get to work. We all hear the business statistics that point to the fact that it takes two years minimum to see a profit on a business. This is more than true in this business. It may often take longer. But that depends on you. Another sad statistic in our industry mentioned earlier is that each year for every two salons that open one closes. We can point often to the fact that beauty professionals are not good businesspeople, but this understanding won't do you any good. You've now embarked on the business and you're going to be a part of a large swing in the statistics to long-term success.

FIGURE 8-1 *The exterior of With Class, A Day Spa, in Tyler, Texas.*

MARKETING

It is interesting to note that most of the true day spas around the country at the time of this writing are doing well. This portends well for the future. Possibly this is true because the day spa owner realizes that to make it now takes constant attention to marketing. But what is marketing and what is the difference between marketing and retailing? And why is it the subject of an entire chapter? Let's look at some definitions for a moment.

According to *Webster's Ninth New Collegiate Dictionary*:

1.	marketing	1: the act or process of selling or purchasing in a market. 2: an aggregate of functions involved in moving goods from producer to consumer.
2.	retailing	the activities involved in the selling of goods to ultimate consumers for personal or household consumption.

There's actually a difference in that marketing includes the selling itself but also all other functions to support the selling. Now we sometimes like to use the word *marketing* to simply mean *retailing* in a nicer, more impressive way. To market this cleanser may sound better than to retail it or even sell it. You see, our profession for some reason has an aversion to selling. Estheticians and massage therapists in particular do not like the connotation associated with retailing or selling. They often want to be considered "above it." Well, the reality is that all we do in this business is some form of selling or retailing, whether it's the product, the service, or the personality of the technician. The marketing is really broader in scope. You can retail that cleanser to the customer, but it's the marketing that gets the customer in the day spa to start with.

So now that we have a better idea of the difference, let's look at the marketing of a day spa with the clear understanding that just because you may have to spend a couple hundred thousand dollars opening a fine, completely equipped facility doesn't mean that you will have clients. The marketing of that day spa tells the ultimate story of your success or failure. And whether you realize it or not now, the marketing never ceases to be important. To bring it all together is an ongoing process. We'll break it up into three major categories: advertising, promotions, and retailing in the spa.

ADVERTISING

Advertising is the process by which you get your spa known and bring in clients (Figure 8-2). There are many ways to advertise, some at no expense and some very expensively. Dividing advertising into the no-charge and paid categories doesn't dismiss either one individually. You must have a balance of both. Additionally, you must make a determination as to whether you want to handle all your own advertising or hire an agency to help you with creation of ads and placement. Ad agencies are often very worthwhile but cost money. They have professional expertise to create advertising programs and develop public relations contacts for added press coverage. If you have a very tight budget, you may want to operate on your own for a while and count on the expertise of the advertising source to help you. Also, study the advertising of your competitors and even beauty-related retail companies for ideas.

FIGURE 8-2 *Consider the effectiveness of this advertising piece for* Day Spa Beautique Salon.

Paid Advertising

YELLOW PAGES

Probably the first thing you will want to do is investigate the value of Yellow Page advertising. You must, of course, have a listing, but whether you should purchase a display or not is difficult to determine. Analyze the advertising in the book, even talk to the other advertisers in your category and inquire about the effectiveness. The difficult determinant is this: you may not receive a million telephone calls, but what if one client sees it, comes in, and becomes a regular client who spends hundreds of dollars a week? Was it worth it? Certainly. One of the options may be to rotate your major advertising budget on and off the telephone book. The down side is if a client happens to notice your ad gone; rumors of closure will also spread, but this isn't a large risk. If you find it effective, obviously keep it going.

NEWSPAPERS

In some communities, newspaper ads are the best form of advertising. The size of the ad and creativity of copy will tell you how effective the advertising program is. Unless you have a large advertising budget, it's better to run 1/4- to 1/2-page ads instead of full pages. An important point to remember in any print ad is that it normally takes three times or more to gain the reader's attention, so placing just one ad in hopes that it will bring you hundreds of clients is unrealistic. Plan a sequence of three or more insertions. Secure the newspaper's recommendations on the best placement in the paper for your type of business. Believe it or not, if you run a special promotional ad for let's say Valentine's Day in the sports section you may be surprised at how many men will purchase gift certificates for their wives or girlfriends. A touch sneaky and even subliminal perhaps but effective.

RADIO AND TELEVISION

Paid advertising in radio and television is more complicated, and thorough research is suggested. If your local area has cable and paid-for talk shows, this may be a good advertising medium for you providing you're good on television. Dr. Mark Lees has hosted a television talk show in Pensacola, Florida, for years. It turned out very well for him. It made him practically an area hero and brought his salon, Mark Lees Skin Care, tremendous business and credibility. It's not to say that it would necessarily work the same way for you in your area. Cable may or may not be available or affordable.

Radio is another interesting medium for advertising. In some areas, radio is very effective. In others, it's either too costly for the number of spots needed to be effective or it's just plain ineffectual. Some people swear by radio and others hate it. You'll have to investigate this more.

SIGNS AND BILLBOARDS

In a small town with one major main street through town, billboard advertising is sometimes phenomenally beneficial. In a large metropolitan area, one sign may not do much good for the cost. It also depends on the location and length of time. The one interesting advantage to a billboard is the free time you'll get if the space isn't sold right away after your contract is completed. Most billboard companies prefer to keep a sign until the next contract is sold so you may have days, weeks, even months of free advertising. Don't count on that, however, for your reason to try it. As for yard signs, whether lit or not, unless you have had great experience, it's not normally recommended. Yard signs are the ones that are driven up to the edge of the street on a trailer and left there to promote something like a restaurant or someone's birthday. It's not very upscale in image.

MAGAZINES, LOCAL AREA PAPERS, SPECIFIED PUBLICATIONS

Most day spas are not prepared to advertise in national magazines such as *Vogue*. One-page ads in those publications cost $35,000 and up. Perhaps your city has a city magazine, such as D *Magazine* in Dallas. These local magazines may be very feasible, but study the demographics and advertising perks available to you. If you purchase advertising, you should receive a certain amount of free editorial coverage as well. Smaller area papers and specific publications may often be very beneficial. (Figure 8-3) In addition to the exposure, it exhibits civic goodwill and may help develop a strong clientele from a public relations standpoint, not just from the ad itself. For example, you may choose to advertise in the local Junior League's charity ball program. If your day spa is upscale, another good avenue for advertising is the programs for the theater, concerts and symphony, and ballet.

---

industry Update

Do you remember when salon skin care amounted to a "good facial", and that was it? In those days, estheticians had little real science to rely on. Instead, they would differentiate themselves with fancy foreign accents, mysterious formulas and techniques. (Ever hear of sheep spleen extract?)

Back then the field suffered from lack of professional standards. Some doctors were reluctant to refer patients to an esthetician, and often poo-pooed the entire industry.

Needless to say, all that has changed. Skin care isn't mysterious any more. It's documented. It's scientific. And it's generating new respect for estheticians who are leading their profession in exciting new directions.

Discoveries such as glycolic acid, free radical fighters and microcurrent technology have finally made it possible to slow down and sometimes reverse the effects of aging. These developments are moving skin care more and more into, and alongside, the field of medicine. They're producing a new kind of esthetician:

* One who dermatologists rely on to develop important treatment methodology for these new substances.
* One who plastic surgeons cooperate with closely, for pre- and post-operative treatments that complement plastic surgery.
* One who partners with the medical profession to provide the patient/client with skin care services which doctors see as beneficial, but for various reasons do not provide in their own practices.
* One that absolutely must be adequately schooled in anatomy, physiology and the science of skin care, in order to properly administer new methods and formulations.

As advanced skin care moves far beyond the facial, it is time for the industry to move away from diversity, and toward the stringent standards of certification that new scientific treatments demand.

David & Mary has been committed to the establishment of strict industry standards since entering the field 14 years ago. In fact, we helped spearhead development of the first board certification standards for estheticians in Indiana. But licensing standards have always varied from state to state.

Now more than ever, there is a need for a higher certification to give clients the assurance they deserve. The industry itself is working to establish a code that identifies highly qualified estheticians, and acts as a reference point for evaluating skin care services.

We thought you'd be glad to know that we at David & Mary are involved. We have been invited, along with other leading skin care experts, to help develop these new certification guidelines. The committee is now hard at work, hammering out the educational, scientific and ethical requirements which will define the all-new esthetician certification examinations.

In time, skin care clients and patients embarking on cosmetic surgery will be able to consult a directory of the country's most educated skin care professionals. Finally, the credo top estheticians have long embraced will be fully articulated. And you will know exactly what you're getting before you walk into a salon.

In the meantime, how do you sort through all the magazine articles, miracle cures, incomplete answers, old wives tales and your own high hopes for fresher, more healthy skin?

We hope you keep coming to David & Mary. Leadership and continued professional integrity are critical components of our service to you.

The science of skin care certainly isn't what it used to be — and that's exactly what we're so enthused about here. Now, as always, we strive to answer your questions in as complete a manner as possible, while we lead our field with skin care solutions that work.

David Miller
Director of Skin Care

DAVID & MARY

Facials • Body Treatments • Nails • Makeup
Nora Corners
1540 East 86th Street
Indianapolis, Indiana 46240
317-844-6662

FIGURE 8-3 *This industry update is informational as well as a direct advertisement for the day spa.*

DONATIONS

Another form of advertising is service donations. For example, the local cancer society is holding a silent auction and you donate a service for the auction. The announcement and description of the treatment is a form of advertising. However, be very careful in your number of charitable donations. You must plan a budget for how many and what you are willing to donate over a period of a year. By doing so, when you get too many calls and requests for donations, you can simply ask the sponsor to send you information in writing for consideration in the budget for the coming year. You can be inundated by your own clients wanting you to donate services and you must guard yourself without seeming stingy to your client.

WORD-OF-MOUTH REWARD SYSTEM

As we all know, the best form of advertising is word of mouth. And although most of that winds up being free to the extent that you may not even know how word is spreading, it's also prudent to offer clients a little something for helping to bring you business. For example, you may want to offer a complimentary service (specify and periodically change it) to clients for every three new clients they send you. And to keep your staff pushing this, you may want to periodically offer a gift or bonus to the staff member who brings in the most new clients in a given period of time.

NOTE: *When offering a complimentary service, never use the word free. Free does not have a professional connotation and sounds cheap.* Complimentary *is a much better word.*

Free Advertising

COMPLIMENTARY TREATMENTS

Another valuable tool to build word-of-mouth advertising in the beginning is to do some complimentary treatments on strategically chosen people. Again, this should be planned out and limited. You can go out of business doing complimentary treatments to build clientele. But some of this is essential in the early development of your day spa. Strategically chosen people might be anyone you feel can provide a great deal of exposure. For example, perhaps you give a massage and hydrotherapy tub treatment to your banker, who's also president of the chamber of commerce. When he tells you how much he loved the treatment, suggest that he mention his wonderful experience to people in the bank and members of the chamber. Do you suppose that will be good advertising? Most likely, yes!

Another valuable source for word-of-mouth advertising is to offer complimentary treatments to members of the press, newspaper, radio, television. Check into the policies of the media in question as many are not allowed to accept a complimentary treatment and may turn down your offer without giving it any further thought. If you know the policy, you have the ability to word your offer differently. Invite the fashion editor out to experience the latest in facial treatments. It's not a complimentary treatment. It's research, so to speak.

While we're on the subject of complimentary treatments, your technicians may be upset at giving away services without being compensated. This can be a large bone of contention if a policy hasn't been established in advance and covered in your policies and procedures manual. When a complimentary service has been properly used, it inures to the benefit of both the spa and the technician. If the spa is willing to offer it, the employee should be willing to give it. There should be an agreed-upon number of complimentary treatments per month. Beyond that, both the owner and employee should be willing to pay their part. Notice I mentioned both. If the employee wants to treat her own mother for free in the spa, if it's over the agreed-upon comps, then the employee should pay the spa's percentage. If, however, the spa owner wants to give a comp over and above the agreed-upon number, then the owner should pay the employee's percentage. This is reciprocal and fair. All complimentary services and products should be determined before the problem arises.

PRESS RELEASES

You may write and mail press releases about your opening, addition of new personnel, to announce new products or treatments, report on advanced education received, report awards or honors received, and so forth. It's always wise to do this as often as possible. The release itself should be typewritten, double spaced, and kept short, no longer than one page. Whenever possible, include a black and white photo (not Polaroid instant photo). You will never know when and if the editors will publish the news. But be aware that all editors need "fillers," items of news to fill holes in the paper or magazine. If your press release is published, you will be surprised at how good the response usually is. Editorial coverage always has more value than paid advertising to the reader. The format for a press release follows.

SHIATSU PRESS RELEASE (Sample)

When writing your release, remember the following:

1. Always write in third person.
2. Send 5 x 7 or 8 x 12 black and white glossy photograph.
3. Never mention your name or your salon name more than twice.
4. Never mention prices.
5. Invite the beauty/fashion editor to your salon for a complimentary treatment.

FOR IMMEDIATE RELEASE: New Oriental Massage

Contact: Name
             Address
             Phone

"MY SALON" NOW OFFERS SHIATSU ORIENTAL MASSAGE

Double Space

Jane Doe of My Salon has just returned from a _____ day intensive workshop on Shiatsu Oriental Massage. Shiatsu is an extremely effective massage technique based on Chinese medical concepts. The instructor, Erica Miller, graduated from the Imai Shiatsu Massage School in Tokyo, Japan. This advanced treatment can benefit stress, pain (headaches), and relaxation.

Shiatsu is now being offered at:

> Your Salon
> Your Address
> Your Town

The real key to making press releases work well for you, particularly if you don't have a PR or ad agent, is to do them well. Every time you go to a seminar, meet someone famous, pass an examination, purchase a new product, anything and everything, always take photos. Then draft your press release on the airplane home and type it up soon. If you don't do it right away, the press release doesn't happen.

You may send them out time and time again to no avail. But one day, it will appear or the beauty editor will remember your day spa and call you for an interview when she's doing a piece on something related. As a true example, this author was quoted in *Vogue* magazine with a one-line mention of my day spa, nothing more. Within about two days of the magazine's release, I was contacted by the Park Cities edition of the *Dallas Morning News*, Dallas' major newspaper. Lo and behold, within a week a full-page article about me and the spa appeared. And it didn't cost me a dime. Now we're called for interviews, and what do think it did for business? That's how it sometimes works. You just never know.

PUBLIC APPEARANCES

If you're shy you must get over it. The opportunities to speak to women's groups, clubs, or schools are everywhere and a wonderful way to build your name without costing money. You may want to introduce yourself and day spa by letter, then make an appointment with the responsible individual to discuss how you might help the organization. Educating the public is a very effective form of advertising. You don't have to push your business on them, just be knowledgeable and personable and care about their needs. As you educate the public, you automatically increase business.

WALK AND TALK IT

Live, eat, and breathe your business everywhere you go. This will be great advertising in and of itself. Carry your business cards and give them out. Have services yourself and talk about the results. Be excited, be verbal, and promote all you can. It will be beneficial. Obviously you believe in the importance and value of your business; tell everyone else.

FIGURE 8-4 *One form of advertisement. Promote your day spa before major holidays, when people are more apt to pamper themselves and/or think of others.*

CHAPTER 8 Marketing and Retailing 119

• •

SPA POINT

There are so many different forms of advertising (Figure 8-4). We've discussed just a few opportunities. You need a good balance between the type of advertising you must pay for and others that are obtainable by good public relations. America thrives on advertising. Be creative or, if you choose to, hire a public relations/ advertising agency to help you build your day spa. Be cautious and choose agencies based upon solid knowledge of their reputation and effective results. Advertising can be fun or a nightmare. It's an ongoing learning process. Don't be afraid to learn and grow.

• •

PROMOTIONS

In this category, we're actually referring to in-spa activities or events to promote your business (Figure 8-5). There is an unwritten rule about making promotions successful: plan them six months to a year ahead and implement them one to two weeks before the department stores. Another good rule of thumb is not to offer a promotion every single month or on all the expected holidays. As David Miller has been quoted as saying, "I don't need to run special Christmas or Mother's Day promotions because I do enough business in gift certificates and packages during that time anyway...I prefer the more obscure times." If you offer monthly or consistent promotions your clientele may grow accustomed to waiting for the specials because they know when to expect them.

The operative words here are *plan* and *implement*. One without the other won't work. *Timing* might be the third word. Day after day I hear war stories from day spa owners about "needing to do that," and yet the usual excuse is lack of time. The sad part to consider in this error is the simple fact that the owner might have more time if the spa were maximizing its potential and promotions were bringing in the dollars. Make proper planning for your promotional activities an absolute must.

At Correlations, all of our classes, shows, and promotional activities are developed during a three-day executive meeting held away from the office, often in a hotel out of state with no phone. Certainly the program changes but since this began about eight years ago, we have stayed 85 percent or more on target. We also prepare for this meeting months ahead by accumulating the information on classes and events and talking to our clients and reps. We have a specific date for promotional launches and these change when new products are introduced. But the point for you to keep in mind is simply the strategic planning part.

Another example is that friend you've been wanting to get together with for dinner but just never seem to get around to it because you're both so busy. What happens if you call and put a date on your calendar? Don't the chances improve dramatically that you will actually get together? And why do you suppose the publisher of this book gave me a deadline?

BEAUTY the MARKS

SKIN CARE MAKE-UP AND FASHION TRENDS

| VOLUME 2 | SPRING/SUMMER, 1989 | NUMBER 1 |

BY THE SEA...

For centuries, people of all ages have been looking to the sea in search of the health, beauty, and special treatments that only seawater can give.

Upon the opening of David & Mary almost three years ago, Indianapolis was first introduced to the world-renowned concept of **thalassotherapy** - a treatment method for toning, tightening, and remineralizing skin. The treatment utilizes baths saturated with lyophilized (freeze-dried) seaweed, body wraps of seaweed and marine mud, specialized massage using marine products, and the thalasso-hydrotherapy tub designed and built in the Brittany region of northern France.

"It was a major decision to import the thalasso tub, but a necessary one for continuing the education of David & Mary clients as to the tremendous revitalizing and rebalancing properties these treatments can have on the entire body," explains salon co-founder David Miller. "It is important to realize that, not only does facial skin need to be kept healthy, but also that of the entire body."

With all the emphasis on better dietary habits and regular exercise, Americans are becoming more aware that proper skin and body care is important as well.

But why seaweed of all things? It's certainly not the most glamorous of beauty products. The truth is, seaweed, or more appropriately - algae - is very high in vitamins, mineral salts, trace elements, and amino acids that contain great hydrating ability. Together, these substances allow more oxygen to nourish the skin cells, leaving it more smooth and supple.

David further explains, "The elements found in seawater, especially the trace elements, can greatly affect our metabolic levels. When our skin becomes low in vitamin and mineral content, the metabolism slows and the pores become clogged, which dries the skin and creates a dull appearance. And while we need to replenish these vitamins and minerals from within by adding them to our diets, skin cells also need to be 'shocked' from their sluggishness. Seaweed-based products, due to their high iodine content, have tremendous activating and accelerating properties which improve circulation and help remove toxins from the body."

Day Spa Spells Relaxation and Revitalization

You've wanted to pamper yourself with a spa visit for some time, but you just can't seem to find the time. Does that sound familiar? If it does, read on, because we know you're busy — too busy to run off to some far away spa for a week.

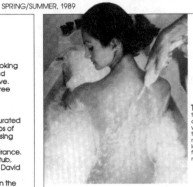

Thalassotherapy treatments utilize baths and body wraps of vitamin-rich seaweed to tone, tighten and remineralize the skin, leaving your entire body feeling pampered and revitalized.

The state-of-the-art treatment that you receive during your body service at David & Mary, whether it's a body facial, body sluffing, thalassic tub treatment, or aromatherapy body massage, is designed to give you an enhanced awareness of your body's needs. So after your short-stay spa program, you'll go home *revitalized*, with a better understanding of how to map out your home body care in conjunction with your other health habits.

In short, you'll receive the same pampering treatments that you would at a world-class spa, but without interrupting your schedule. And your attitude will improve dramatically. It's an attitude that our European friends have held for years - that taking a little time out of each day to *relax* allows you to function at a better level, stay healthier, and possibly live a longer, more fulfilling life.

Why not try it? You've got nothing to lose...and a great deal to gain!

The following is a list of Spa Services available at David & Mary:

Herbal Paraffin Body Facial

The ultimate in warm paraffin treatments for the entire body. Aromatic oils are selected according to your skin condition and lightly massaged into the skin. The body is then painted with several layers of warm paraffin wax, followed by a protective coating, a sheet and a warm blanket. Warming lights activate the oils to help hydrate, detoxify, and purify the skin as your body is soothed and relaxed — head to toe!

(continued on page 4)

FIGURE 8-5 *You can compose your own newsletter as a way of promoting and advertising your day spa. Consider how often you would need to publish it.*

. . . .

SPA POINT

There is absolutely no way to develop an effective promotional program for your day spa unless you plan it and implement it according to a reasonable time schedule.

. . . .

Types of Promotions

SEASONAL

These are the simplest. Just follow the big seasonal events (Figure 8-6). Now the trick to making Christmas, Easter, Halloween, and others really pay off is to match or beat the department stores to the punch. If you have your Christmas promotion developed, Christmas decorations ready, gift certificates and package gifts ready, get them out right after Halloween. I see so many grumbling spa owners finally decorating on December 10. It's way too late. Your best selling time is the month before and then the week before Christmas. Some day spas mail out Santa Wish Lists naming services and products that husbands can purchase for their wife and vice versa. Then the spa handles the wrapping. That's a great promotion.

IRREGULAR

These are the more obscure dates, perhaps the anniversary of the spa opening, the date of your successful passing of the CIDESCO International Exam, or just a day of happiness in the spa. These should be unique and never repeated year after year.

GWPs AND PWPs

These were briefly discussed in chapter 7. To review the terminology: GWP means gift with purchase, for example, purchase a six-week series of deep hydrating facial treatments and receive a special hydrating serum, retail value $65 (always good to show the retail value). PWP means purchase with purchase. When you purchase something for a certain amount, you have the opportunity to purchase something else at a drastically reduced price (Figure 8-7).

These are common with the upscale department store lines. However, they are so much larger than most of the professional companies and day spas that I believe Dr. Mark Lees defines the practical use in our industry quite well. He explains, "I can't afford to give away a $15 makeup bag by itself as a GWP, so I offer it at say $10 (just a little over my cost to cover freight, etc.) if a client purchases three Mark Lees products." This works well because the point of the PWP is to sell the three products, but we know the makeup bag is attractive and will encourage interest. The client may not have really intended to buy three products, but the bag becomes the incentive.

You may want to choose your PWP items from your own product lines and accessories or go out to gift market to find some. But be careful and don't overbuy. A salon owner client once purchased some gold makeup bags thinking they'd go like hotcakes. They didn't and it took her nearly three years to get rid of them. She couldn't just dump them because she was in a small town and the first ones were given as special promotions. Dumping them would have devalued them and made the clients look unimportant. So be careful and when in doubt, underestimate your needs for GWPs and PWPs, but be sure to do them periodically.

FIGURE 8-6 *Holiday promotions offering specials, gifts, or discounts are great ways to advertise your services and get new clients.*

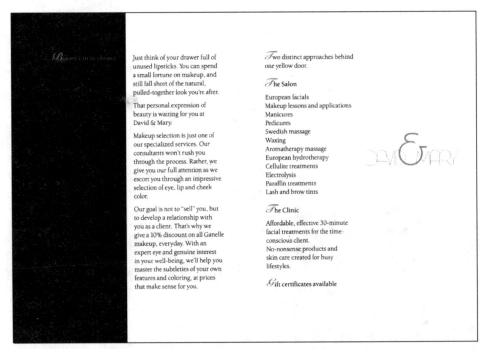

Just think of your drawer full of unused lipsticks. You can spend a small fortune on makeup, and still fall short of the natural, pulled-together look you're after.

That personal expression of beauty is waiting for you at David & Mary.

Makeup selection is just one of our specialized services. Our consultants won't rush you through the process. Rather, we give you our full attention as we escort you through an impressive selection of eye, lip and cheek color.

Our goal is not to "sell" you, but to develop a relationship with you as a client. That's why we give a 10% discount on all Ganelle makeup, everyday. With an expert eye and genuine interest in your well-being, we'll help you master the subtleties of your own features and coloring, at prices that make sense for you.

Two distinct approaches behind one yellow door.

The Salon

European facials
Makeup lessons and applications
Manicures
Pedicures
Swedish massage
Waxing
Aromatherapy massage
European hydrotherapy
Cellulite treatments
Electrolysis
Paraffin treatments
Lash and brow tints

The Clinic

Affordable, effective 30-minute facial treatments for the time-conscious client.
No-nonsense products and skin care created for busy lifestyles.

Gift certificates available

FIGURE 8-7 *Offer discounts on products if clients receive related treatments. Here, David & Mary build up their 10 percent discount on makeup.*

EMULATE TRENDS

Another avenue for terrific ideas is advertisements found in magazines and on television. The big companies have ad and PR agencies, lawyers, and the like developing their campaigns, and they spend millions of dollars. You may not have the same resources to develop yours so why not look to the retail industry for some ideas. This is not to suggest plagiarism or stealing, just learning and researching. An interesting thing for you to consider that often comes up in my classes is that estheticians today are still concentrating their retail efforts on cleanser, freshener, and moisturizer. There's nothing wrong with this, but the reality is that the consumer is looking more for the specialty items: serums, "anti-aging" miracle juice, and the like. If you have the types of products that your customer sees advertized daily in the consumer magazines or on television, don't you suppose that your version of that would be a rather easy sell? Remember when clear mascara was the rage? Well, if you had it then, you certainly sold a lot. If you didn't, you missed a lot of money.

This awareness of the media is part of a good promotional mindset. And from your clients' standpoint, whatever appears in print "must be true" (even if it's not), so an up-to-date, alive, alert day spa stays on top of those trends or dispels myths too. And this is what keeps that client excited about your business.

. . . .

SPA POINT

Estee Lauder herself may be credited with making the GWP concept work so well and it's been done for decades since in retail. Although the professional salon industry is different and because we want to think of ourselves as better and more professional than this, and we are, we're still in the retail and promotional business. Watch those magazines, department stores, and cosmetic lines to get ideas. And then the mandate for the businessperson in a day spa is to implement them cleverly. A well-done promotion is not only profitable but exciting for the clients. An exciting alive day spa keeps a clientele.

RETAILING

FIGURE 8-8 *Retailing is important for two reasons: it brings in more revenue and it provides clients with further individualized attention.*

As stated in the definitions at the beginning of this chapter, retailing is the process of selling products to the end user. An excellent book specifically addressing retailing for this industry is *SalonOvations: It's In the Bag*, by Carol Phillips, published by Milady Publishing Company. Therefore, we will not discuss specific retailing techniques. Rather let's look at retailing more as an operational issue. But don't fail to study Phillips' book. It has to be a very important part of your business if you want to survive and prosper.

Now, let's be blunt (I'm known for this): we, licensed professionals, tend to think we're above the need to retail. We don't want to be equated with the counter person in a department store or a car dealer. We're licensed professionals after all. The statistics on service to retail percentages in this industry at the time of writing this book are not good. Retailing has improved in recent years because products have improved and because we've finally realized that it's not only a money-making proposition but also is essential to properly care for the client (Figure 8-8).

Now here's the other rub. Even though all the segments of the profession should be cross-selling each other's services and products to some extent, the tendency for the hairdresser is to ignore skin and for the body therapist to ignore face, and vice versa. Probably the only one easily promoted by all is the makeup artist, because after all, most women wear makeup. The point here is to state emphatically that the whole idea of the day spa is total body care that includes hair, skin, nails, body, and makeup. It must be a team effort, and all departments must retail to properly care for the client (Figure 8-9). It's not just peddling products, it's fulfilling our responsibility to ensure that the client maintains the proper home care while receiving our professional treatments. It doesn't do any good to have a great perm if the client goes home and washes her hair that night with an over-the-counter high alkaline shampoo, or to have a great facial only to follow up at home with a bar of soap or laundry detergent because if it's good enough for the clothes it must be okay for the face. Don't these practices negate to a large extent the benefits of the professional treatment received? Certainly!

The only reason consumers purchase their beauty products in the department, drug, or grocery store is because we let them get away. It is the very strong opinion of this author that all beauty products should be purchased in the day spa, never on the open retail market. (Figure 8-10) So in the same vein, consider the importance of only retailing professional lines. Every now and again we'll see direct sales lines being sold out of a salon or

FIGURE 8-9 *Do you advertise and promote your retailing efforts as well as your treatments?*

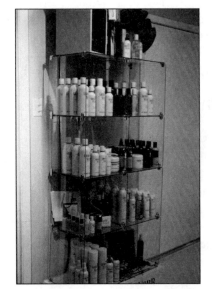

FIGURE 8-10 *Are your retail products prominently displayed and easily accessible to clients?*

Operational Retail Issues

day spa. Why would you want to compete with your own customer? How can this support the difference between your professional license and the retailer? A wise consideration for you is to sell only lines that are strictly marketed in the professional beauty industry.

. . . .

SPA POINT

Retailing is not really an option but a must for the professional day spa. If a client cares enough to go there for services, you must care enough to be sure the home care program is properly done. And as you must know, what the client does at home twice a day thirty or so times a month is far more important than what you may do a couple of times a month. Take care of retailing; it's part of your professional job.

. . . .

There are some interesting aspects of retailing, normally not taken into consideration. First of all, how do you, the spa owner, expect your staff to retail well for you if they don't use the product themselves? Why do you book your technicians too tightly to be able to retail when the known profitability of the business is really in retail? In this section, we'll look at some of the most common retailing problems from an in-house standpoint.

STAFF EXPERIENCES

Make sure that all staff, including receptionist, has personally experienced every treatment available in all departments and takes notes on the key selling points of each. Since this is a somewhat costly thing to do for the owner, it's suggested that the employee be tested or required to be able to sell the treatments back to you. A lot of fun variations of this practice should be done, preferably prior to the initial opening and then during the training period for all new employees.

STAFF DISCOUNTS

Allow the staff to purchase products at a substantial discount, barely over your cost (including freight). If you don't want the employee to know your costs, develop your employee price structure as a discount percentage off retail. A suggestion might be to sell to your staff at 35 percent off (assuming your discount from retail is 50 percent). This discount shouldn't pass on down to second cousins twice removed; keep it in the employee's immediate family.

Do staff incentive promotions from time to time and give products, preferably products they haven't tried. If you'll take advantage of options like supplier specials and baker's dozens (the free thirteenth one for an order of twelve), you will have products to work with at no cost to you. But even if it costs you a little it's worth it in the long run.

STAFF KNOWLEDGE

Work as a team and be knowledgeable about all department's services and products to as great an extent as possible without displacing the expert in that department. Don't ever say, "I don't know anything about hair." Ask the hairdresser. Talk about how great your hair services are and suggest a hairdresser to consult with the client to determine the specific needs. Discuss retail products to the extent you can and then turn the sale over to the person handling that area.

THINK IN RETAIL DOLLARS, NOT WHOLESALE

This goes for the owner as well as the hands-on technicians. You may know that cream actually costs $35, but the retail price on it is $70. It's natural for you to feel in your heart that it's only really worth $35, but you must not. When you buy products yourself in other industries, you have no problem thinking in their retail figures. Your clients have no trouble thinking of that cream at $70. When you create promotions or give gifts, remember the value of that product at retail, not wholesale.

PRICING

As the technician who perhaps makes 10 percent commission on that $70 cream, it's also easy to feel like you can't afford it, so the client probably can't either. After all, you'd have to sell ten of those creams to be able to buy one at retail, so it's too expensive. This is a totally self-defeating concept. First of all, we must never assume that a client can't afford anything.

We can all afford what we consider a priority, no matter what. We don't know the client's priorities. We never know what the client wants to spend and what products will sell. As a result, if you believe in your products and believe truthfully that the client will benefit, you have a responsibility to present all of them. Assumption is a retail killer.

CLIENT PRICE RESISTANCE

You responsibly present a complete set of products, and let's say that the total comes to $120. This may sound high to you, but then the client seems a little hesitant too, so your own reticence jumps in and you want to back off. Think it out again and try presenting this to the client: if an average set of products lasts about two months, then the actual per-day cost is only $2. That's less than a hamburger and french fries. Can your client, who cared enough to partake in your excellent and effective services, afford $2 a day for the only skin she will ever get? Certainly. Again, your job is to believe in the value of your home care and assume that the client will purchase products from you, not the department store; $2 per day is nothing, so breaking the cost of items to per-day usage is a viable way to reduce the price resistance. The main point here for your consideration is who's really hesitating, the client or you?

STAFF RESISTANCE

"Oh, who cares, retailing is too much trouble and I don't make enough on it anyway!" This problem is rampant. It's very helpful for the spa owner to nip this in the bud, not by forcing retailing and threatening to fire the employee, per se, but rather by showing the employee how much that 10 percent can amount to over a month's period. In questioning day spas, we find that good retailers can easily make $500 to $1,000 or more per month in commissions, particularly on graduated scales for volume. It's really not unusual to make sales in the multiple hundreds of dollars to an individual client anyway. And all the while you're making that money, the client ownership is solidified, the effectiveness and results of the treatments are enhanced, and the whole machine works as it should.

BOOKINGS AND COMMISSIONS

"I'm booked so solid, I don't have time to retail, I can't get out of the room, and I never get the commission on a rebuy if my client just happens to come in for something so why bother?" From an employee standpoint, you still have the responsibility to sell anyway in order to properly care for the client, irrespective of the booking situation or front desk sales policy. Owners, these are two very strong retail killers. If the employee is booked so tightly that there's no time to discuss retail with the client, the client loses the benefit of proper advice, and you lose the income from retail. Remember that retail, not service, is the heart of the business profits. You must allow time for the technician to sell. If your operation is big enough, you may want to hire a helper to do the cleanup and setup, particularly necessary in wet areas. This frees your technician to sell. Now you will, of course, train that technician to take the time to talk retail with the client, not wander off to the break room.

As for the commission on a client who comes in, this is a tricky issue. If the technician hasn't bothered to talk to the client about retail, why should you commission him/her? On the other hand, you can't expect the client to always purchase at the moment the product was discussed, nor can you know for sure that the employee isn't following up on repurchases. This is a judgment call for you, but it's suggested that the technicians always be commissioned on their clients no matter what. If someone walks in off the street and the front desk sells something, that might be considered a house account. If you have a front desk retail person, you may have to consider some split commissions or incentives. That makes the issue more complicated. But a technician should never be penalized for the inability to make a sale while working on someone else. If you do, it will most certainly kill the technician's incentive to sell and your profits will reflect this. Just to keep that 10 percent at the front desk on a few sales at the cost of the many sales by the technician isn't worth it.

And finally, owners should ascertain a prospective employee's attitude about retail during the interview process. If the person is totally negative about retailing for any reason, you may want to consider hiring someone else.

. . . .

SPA POINT

There are so many little operational issues from the owner to the employee that can seriously hinder quality retailing, from booking the employee too close together to having a bad attitude about retailing. Everything and everybody in the day spa must think retail at all times. This doesn't mean a hard sell approach, but it does mean attention to details and not assuming anything about the client. Everyone must be excited about the products and their effects, the atmosphere must be conducive to quality selling, and the whole crew must be excited and recognize the benefits of retail.

. . . .

FIGURE 8-11 *Nail, skin, and hair products should all be displayed in an area frequented by all your clients. This makes your day spa more conducive to retailing opportunities.*

Is the Day Spa Conducive to Retailing?

This is so important (Figure 8-11). Are all your products locked up in cabinets behind the check-out desk to prevent stealing? Do you buy hand soap in bulk from Sam's for the dispensers in the bathrooms? Do you have one very dusty product display on the premises? Does your client literature consist of *People* magazine and the *National Inquirer*? Perhaps you're amused right now, but these and more are common problems.

YOU SELL WHAT YOU USE

Even though it may be somewhat expensive, it's more effective to have your products available for use in the bath and locker rooms. Why in the world would you put out a product you specifically sell against? Your sales will far outweigh the cost.

FIGURE 8-12 A *retail display should be neat, stocked, and attractive.*

LET CLIENTS TRY PRODUCTS

Are your products locked up, testers glued to the display so that the client can only look at them? Let's be realistic, and think of the department store. It's a known fact that sales improve dramatically when the client is able to see, touch, smell, experience. Yes, you will have some theft, but that's all part of the cost of doing business. Again, sales will far outweigh the cost.

DISPLAYS

How are your displays? (Figure 8-12) Do you even have any? Are they loaded with product and moved around every four to six weeks? If not, they should be. There is a very practical reason why shelves in department store cosmetic areas are packed; it sells. Nobody wants to purchase the last one of anything. And dust, hair trimmings, hair spray, and the like on the shelves and products should be against the law. It is a tremendous turnoff and very unprofessional, not to mention unsanitary. Are the makeup displays filthy? Are matted and dirty makeup brushes in a jar on the counter and are mascara wands intact on the mascara? This is a sure way to kill makeup sales. Brushes should be freshly cleaned and prepared between clients and all mascara wands cut off in the containers. Serious cross-contamination can occur, which is a good avenue to spread eye infection; you'll lose the client forever. All makeup, including the lipsticks, should be used with disposable applicators. Are the retail products touchable? It will increase sales. Statistics point to the fact that perhaps as much as 70 percent of retail is impulse, done at checkout. Again, this is proven by the way department, drug, and grocery stores are designed. How about your day spa?

. . . .

SPA POINT

It's sometimes the little things like soap dispensers and dirty shelves or tools that can lose a client, without our knowledge. A professional day spa is built

FIGURE 8-13 *Every area displaying the professional products used in your day spa should be clean and conducive to retailing.*

for and maintained with retail emphasis in mind, from sanitary procedures and cleanliness to product displays that are conducive to selling (Figure 8-13). Clients will not only appreciate the importance and emphasis placed on retail, but will also feel secure in obtaining your services and products. There's really no need for the client to buy anywhere but from you if you've kept your presentation professional and client driven.

· ·

Synopsis

This chapter doesn't even attempt to cover the subject of retailing techniques and skills. Carol Phillips' book is a must to help you with that. In the meantime, just evaluating and placing serious importance on retail consciousness in your salon display and presentation and with your employees can make the difference in thousands upon thousands of dollars in revenue. Each of the issues mentioned in this chapter are absolutely real problems out there. And each is so easy to correct. If you're just starting your day spa handle all of this with education. Retail is, and should be, a vital concern for each and every member of your team. Retail is the heart of the day spa business!

Review

1. What can we point to to understand why one out of two salons annually goes out of business?

2. What is the definition of marketing and what are the important words in that definition?

3. List a few avenues of paid-for advertising.

4. What is the best form of advertising?

5. Should you give unlimited service donations? Why?

6. How often should a press release be sent to the print media?

7. Why is it important for you to live and breathe your business?

8. What are the two operative words related to in-house promotions and why?

9. As professionals is it a mistake to think we're above retailing? Why?

10. Is retailing an option or a must for the day spa?

11. Should the staff be knowledgeable in all departments of the day spa?

12. Why is it important to value products at retail value?

13. Is it okay to book a technician back to back? Why?

14. How should a makeup display look?

15. If you make your entire day spa retail conducive, how should the clients feel?

CHAPTER 9
Where to Go after the First Year _____

OVERVIEW

This chapter will concentrate briefly on concerns after the first successfully completed year. The reality is that many of the points contained herein are still valid from day one, but the most important thing for you to remember after you've made it the first year is not to slack off as so many do. In the experience of the author, more than 70 percent of the businesses begin to slack off after the first year. In extreme cases, a spa that was going great guns the first year begins to die the second year, for no real reason except the erroneous conclusion on the part of the staff or owner that they've "made it," or are too tired to work as hard. As has been said over and over again, this industry is labor intensive and requires a lot of hands-on management. You simply can't let go after the first year. You must maintain your momentum and excitement. If the owner begins to let go and loses momentum, what do you think the employees will do?

Let's touch on just a few primary areas that are of great ongoing concern to the day spa success. The aggregate of all and more is vital, but these points have been chosen from detailed research into day spa weaknesses after the first year.

INVENTORY CONTROL

How's your inventory control system at this point? Have you been doing regular physical inventory? Are you controlling your inventory by computer? Have you allowed your staff to bring in too many bits and pieces of many lines? Are your cabinets full of stuff that isn't being used properly? (Figure 9-1)

Ordering

If you have been able to track your purchases for the first year, you should have a good idea of what is selling and how often you should order. Many day spas place small orders once or twice a week. At this point it's time to graduate to a better system. In the first place, you spend extra money in freight if you place small orders too often. Also, many suppliers offer freight discounts on larger purchases; sometimes it's even free. This can save you hundreds of dollars per year. Some suppliers ship with a "baker's dozen" concept. Remember, this means you receive a free one for every twelve ordered. That free one can represent substantial dollars over the course of a year. And finally, ordering once a month reduces your paperwork and makes inventory control easier. It also makes your suppliers happier and more willing to do little extras for you.

Hopefully by this time you have a good idea of what you need and can project your needs better. Ordering at the last minute with overnight deliv-

 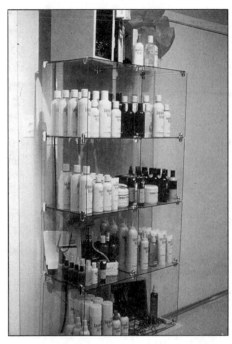

FIGURE 9-1 *Take a good look at your inventory control system. Is it effective? Do you really know what you have in inventory?*

FIGURE 9-2 *How many professional product lines do you currently carry?*

ery or second day air costs you money. If you just tell a client you're out, you're potentially sending that client to your competition. It's certainly still possible to have a run on something and run out but it shouldn't happen too much. If you are computerized, you should program it to kick out a requisition when you're down to three of any item.

Too Many Lines

Have you allowed new incoming staff to convince you that you need another line? Have you wound up with five hair lines or four skin care lines? Back up and take a strong look at this issue (Figure 9-2). Some technicians will hire on telling you that they must have a certain line, so you run out and buy it. Then six months later, the employee is gone but the products aren't. And when this happens over and over, you wind up with thousands of dollars tied up and no continuity. It is certainly advisable to discuss the potential addition of a new line or product with your staff and to obtain their views, but remember that it's your day spa and it's your money. It's your liability when a reaction occurs and nobody knows what line caused the problem. And it's your loss when you have your money spread so thin that you can't take advantage of supplier perks.

And one final very important issue related to this. A spa that's not doing well in a department or overall often wants to place the blame on the product line, thinking if only they had this line or that line, it will all be okay. This is erroneous. As important as your product line is, the ability to sell it and make it work is your responsibility. As suppliers we see this product hopping a lot. The reality is that it won't solve your problem and only increases your inventory nightmare. As an aside, most suppliers also begin to back off spas that are constantly hopping from one line to another. They don't have time to continue helping a business that they only see the potential of losing anyway. Product loyalty is something you demand from your clients so think about it on your side. This is not to say that you should never add products. You should and will, but the motivation must be different.

Product Guarantees

As you will learn, clients may bring products back to you because of reactions, problems with the product, change of mind, irate husbands, and a myriad of reasons often not terribly valid. You will need to develop a policy on this after some experience. Some choose to always take the product back for any reason, some only for reactions and product problems. This can be a touchy subject. One method that seems to work well is to offer a 100 percent guarantee on the product safety (against reactions) when selling it. In reality few people take advantage of that unless they really have a problem. If the product comes back due to a reaction or problem, most suppliers also happily take it back.

The reality, though, is that there are rarely product problems. The reaction is the client not the product. (Some can't eat seafood, but seafood is not bad for all.) You can then choose to send it back to your supplier or just use it in treatment or for display. Take care of the client. Now, the client who uses all but a drop at the bottom and then claims a problem is a little different. You will discover that this client pulls this trick often. First time take it back and make big notes on the chart/records. Second time, it might be well to refuse. If the client gets mad and leaves you, that's fine too. Let your competition deal with it. Be sure your staff is well trained in how to handle product claims (Figure 9-3).

FIGURE 9-3 *Spend the extra time training your staff in how to retail professional products and how to deal with customer service issues.*

Mail Order Products

Although you can set up your business for mail order from day one, it's often difficult the first year until the other basic issues are taken care of and the dust has settled. But from year two on find someplace in your day spa where you can set up a little gift wrapping and shipping area. There is no reason why you can't sell clients products by mail. If you accept credit cards (which you should), purchasing a few boxes, a roll of tape, mailing labels, and packing bubbles is no big deal. The amount of money you can make in mail order will astonish you. No elaboration is necessary. Try it; you'll be shocked. But of course, you must promote the service. And if your employees are doing their follow-ups correctly, mail order should grow well. Look in your Yellow Pages for packing materials. It's not a difficult process to set up and the space needed is minimal.

Supplier Specials

When a supplier offers a special, discount, or extra items often you ignore it thinking you don't need that item right then. Also, you may again be thinking in wholesale dollars and may not realize how much money that special might be worth to you. Sometimes it's worth being a little overstocked for a short time to take advantage of a special. Look at each one from a dollar standpoint, not just how many you have on hand.

. . . .

SPA POINT

Inventory control is a major issue, particularly once you understand how your product flow is going. This area should be analyzed from time to time to be sure you are taking advantage of all the best possibilities. And above all, don't clog up your day spa with too little of too many things. That's a business disaster.

. . . .

SERVICE ISSUES, CONSUMER AND EMPLOYEE

Quality

It's so easy to get caught up in the tyranny of the urgent and forget to observe the ongoing quality of your service. Periodically you must step outside of your day spa and look at it as a customer would. Now, this is most difficult if this is the place you spend eight to twelve hours a day. If you can't, then it's a great idea to obtain a few "mystery shoppers." One only is really not fair. That person may get bogged down in one issue. One person will have only one viewpoint. The mystery shoppers could be friends, distant family members, or even strangers you hire. You may choose to pay for this research in cash or in trade for services. You may want to create a form that the mystery shopper uses to keep on track and look at the issues you want concentrated on, issues such as receptionist friendliness and helpfulness, salon cleanliness, technician professionalism, and follow-through to retail. In addition to yourself and your mystery shoppers, you should ask your very own clients. Don't be afraid of their criticism. No matter what style they reply in, take it as valuable information, and then just ignore what's not applicable.

Addressing Client Needs

"The most fun part for me is seeing a client leave happy feeling that we cared about them. Nothing is more rewarding than to see and hear a client say, 'I had a wonderful time.'"—Kathy Driscoll, The Spa at the Houstonian, Houston, Texas

This is certainly not an issue just after the first year, but you will find some changes after the first year. There's an interesting problem that occurs; whatever you did in the beginning that may have appeared to be "above and beyond" soon becomes the norm and is expected by the client. Then their expectations begin to rise. You can't spend your business life one-upping the last one. You must realistically look at their expectations and what you can do. For example, if you always served brewed gourmet coffee in the beginning and then later put in a coffee machine, what does that do to the client's expectations? What happens when in your new beginning zeal you take 1-3/4 hours for a 1-hour massage or body treatment? How do you cut back now that you're busy? It's a very difficult problem. You will have to re-create and rename that treatment. As you go down the road, and add and change, always consider the ramifications to your clients.

Employee Apathy

This is the most common problem with time in the day spa. How do you continually keep your employees excited and motivated? Realistically you can't, but you must try and this involves keeping the spa itself alive, on top of everything, creating and developing promotions. In addition, staff education is critical. Staff concerns must also be addressed in the same manner as clients'. Remember your staff is human, too. If you didn't have regular staff meetings in the first year, you should begin doing this, whether it's monthly or quarterly, and they should be mandatory. This should be covered in the policies and procedures manual. Don't let those meeting become gripe sessions. Do a lot of different things, education sometimes, promotion creations, just a nice dinner, whatever. Don't let the meetings themselves become so boring that the staff dreads them. You want the staff eager to attend and be recharged as a result.

Client Records/ Follow-Up

In conjunction with employee issues, are your employees following up on the clients? After a treatment are the records up-to-date in the chart or on computer? If there was something specific about the client's skin or hair or nails that should prompt a follow-up call to see how the client's doing, did the technician do it? Does the technician call the client to ask how he/she liked the sample? Are birthday cards sent if that's a policy? Are clients notified if you haven't seen them for a while? Follow-up is absolutely imperative and can take an ordinary day spa and turn it into a highly profitable enterprise by a little extra attention to details. The owner should spot-check this area from time to time to be sure it's up to par. And again, good follow-up will tie in well to your mail order program. If your employees are in good communication and are aware of the client's needs, a tremendous amount of business can take place between visits. Why do you think the mail order and cable television business is so strong? You can fulfill that need very easily.

Watch Your Operation

Keep your belt tightened, analyze your monthly financial statements, stay on budget, and keep those management goals polished. Are you all (entire staff) living up to your mission statement? You must pay ongoing attention to the business side of your business. If you are a working owner and also do services, you'd better plan on scheduling specific time for all the business activities. Many a day spa has gone out of business or just lost profitability because the owner is spending too much time just doing services to try to hold it together. You can't stick your finger in the dike and expect that to hold the dam up, can you?

EDUCATION

FIGURE 9-4 *It is crucial that your staff receive training on a regular basis, whether as a review or to teach a new technique.*

This may be the third topic here but it's certainly not the least important. As a supplier, there's an interesting correlation between education and sales, that is, the day spas that retail well and purchase a lot of products from the supplier consistently attend a lot of product classes. Without exception in this author's computer tracking, my best spas are the ones that put a great deal of emphasis and importance on education and particularly product knowledge. For those out there who have been licensed for a long time or have been using a specific product line for ages, there's often a tendency to feel that you know it well enough and ongoing classes aren't necessary. There are estheticians and massage therapists in the field who brag about how they know it all and don't need any more training. Owners, if anyone says this to you, it's almost a guarantee that there's something he/she absolutely doesn't know.

This industry is growing and evolving at breakneck speed. The product technology is phenomenal. A person who hasn't been updated in the last five years is antiquated in this author's opinion. The technician may not even have a clue what he/she doesn't know and, therefore, doesn't care. But the reality is that the consumer does. The consumer may know it incorrectly but still is far more educated than the antiquated technician may realize. There are also the insecure technicians who know they don't know so the trick is to block training so that no one discovers the lack of knowledge. This is not as uncommon as you might think.

The solution to this is simple—training, training, and more training. Your staff must be educated (Figure 9-4). And both sides must have an interest in this. You must have mandatory product knowledge at the very least. You must encourage your staff to attend advanced education. If you refuse to ever allow an employee time off to attend a class or a show, you are contributing to the process of antiquation yourself. This is not to say that you have to pay for everything. You can and should contribute in any number of ways. You may create special in-house sales promotions for a trip to a show, or help by allowing the employee to have the time off, or even by helping to pay part of the expenses. But you must be totally behind education. And when your suppliers offer to come in to do a lecture or a class make the most of it. If they ask for a time to meet with the entire staff together and have a good program that appears worthwhile, do it. The loss in a few hours of service income may turn out to double or triple income.

And you must also continue your own education in all subjects. You must stay up-to-date with business trends in the industry, computer advances, and management systems. You should attend as many of the classes your staff attends as possible so that you are a knowledgeable boss. Technicians sometimes have a problem by discounting the intelligence of the owner, particularly if the owner is only handling the business. Even if the owner isn't licensed and doesn't perform the services, education in all departments will help keep you in control of your business. If you are a technician owner, you need to stay on top of both technical issues and business issues. Does this tell you that you probably must not work behind the chair every day yourself? As time goes on, the working owner will do well to pass on a large part of the clientele to the staff and designate a large part of the time to running the business. Trying to run the business at night after a long busy day results in lack of quality, inconsistency, fatigue, and improper attention to business.

. . . .

SPA POINT

It's hard to weigh the value of ongoing education immediately and directly, but it certainly does pay off. It will show in the bottom line. Ongoing education is not just a nice perk but an absolute must. Day spas heavily involved in ongoing product knowledge classes invariably sell more. You can never underestimate the power of ongoing education for your staff and for you as well. The owner must keep up-to-date and set a great example for the staff. The owner is, in fact, a role model to the staff, good, bad, or otherwise.

. . . .

THE NEW THINGS

As important and exciting as it is to add new things, you must be pragmatic and careful about what, how, and when new things are added. This is a fast-moving business and clients are always wanting to know what's new. Estheticians are constantly looking for new treatments, masks, techniques. Hairdressers and makeup artists must constantly be aware of new styles. Nail technicians and body therapists must be aware of the latest technology, ingredients, and supplies. In other words, everyone must keep up with the technology and add where applicable and appropriate. But the key is to add new things with proper planning and attention to details.

As we discussed earlier, your clients always want whatever is new. The down side to having something new every other day is how to keep up with it. Isn't it the same with raising a child? If you are constantly bringing home toys, and each time bigger and better ones, what will you do in a few years? You cannot operate a business based only on "new things." Deciding what and how to add is always a great challenge. It may help to make a promotional plan for the year in advance. Sometimes surprises come out and you'll have to readjust, but the key to the entire issue of new things is planning. And new things don't always have to be a new product or treatment. It can be new knowledge, new staff, and even perhaps a new paint job or remodel (not in your second year). It may even be a series of educational programs geared for your clients or open houses.

"The most fun is making everyone feel good. It's fun to perform services and educate clients."—Leah Kovitz, New Image by Leah, Tucson, Arizona

If it does happen to be a product or a new service really build it up in advance of the launch and then milk it as long as possible to keep the excitement going. Also, it's useful to keep in the back of your mind that the average client visits the day spa once every four to six weeks, so plan your launches accordingly. This is why it's great to announce it in advance and then work with it as a special treat for a couple of months to be sure the client is properly exposed to it. And finally, don't get so hooked on the new things that you forget about the old tried and true. It's important to maintain your basic consistent sellers.

ADVISERS

In many of the chapters of this book we've talked about using the services of different experts in their fields, from the day spa consultant to the public relations agency. It's wise to have a team of experts you can refer to on an ongoing basis. Some members of this team may cost money, some shouldn't. Develop a good resource of professional friends in the industry. (You'll make these friends at shows and classes.) Some day spas even have boards of directors or advisory boards to help with the major issues. There's too much involved in a day spa to be able to do it all yourself. The successful and wise business owner taps the resources, continues learning, and never stops.

. . . .

SPA POINT

New is great but can put you into a frenzy trying always to have something new. Something new doesn't necessarily have to be a product. "New things" can be ideas, client programs, newsletters, or remodeling. The crux of the issue is good planning and strategically targeting the new things when it's really wise. You will never be able to keep up if you constantly have to have something new and different. Don't let your client dictate this. You must be in control. Advisers will also be very helpful on an ongoing basis with information, ideas, and suggestions. The good businessperson utilizes all the resources possible at all times.

. . . .

Synopsis

Without a doubt, the successful day spa will be a facility where ongoing training, activity, and employee concern are constantly taking place. The spa may do well the first year and die thereafter due merely to lack of attention to the details that were important in the beginning. Watch your inventory controls and don't count on new products coming into a show to solidify the profitability of your business. Your business must have a stable, well-"oiled" base from which to grow. Education of your staff is the key to maintaining momentum. Keep product and business motivation classes going forever. Keep your employees at the top of their field and care for them as you do for your clients and you.

Review

1. Is it common for day spa businesses to slack off after the first year? Why?

2. How can you improve on your ordering procedures after you've been tracking them for a while?

3. What are some of the advantages of purchasing once a month instead of once or twice a week?

4. Is it possible to have too many lines? What is one problem?

5. Is mail order out of a day spa a viable retail avenue?

6. For what is a "mystery shopper" good?

7. What are some things to do to avoid employee apathy?

8. What are a few major reasons ongoing education is important?

9. What is a problem associated with always trying to add "new things"?

10. Is it important to have advisers after the business has been established?

Answers to Review Questions _____

CHAPTER 1

1. The term *day spa* came from the idea of a facility where the services of a destination spa could be obtained on a short-term basis, in a day or less instead of a lengthy stay. What makes the day spa is the combinations of modalities and the treatments that can be offered. How the combinations are packaged, how the day spa is designed, and how it is presented is what will really make the day spa successful.

2. Water and body treatments are the two most important factors to make a facility a true day spa.

3. Name any one of the seven client types discussed and give personal reasons why you want to concentrate on this group.

CHAPTER 2

1. A beauty salon is ideally suited to day spa development because it's already in the business of improving clients' appearances and how they feel about themselves, and most of the treatment facilities are intact or easily added.

2. An electrolysis clinic is a good spot because clients already care about their appearance, and the facility is nearly set up anyway.

3. A fitness center is the ideal location for series-based services because the client visits the fitness center to exercise several times a week anyway.

4. Yes, a retirement center can do well as a day spa if it's in an affluent environment. The resident is also very conscious of the value of hydrotherapy and body massage, particularly the aging baby boomer.

CHAPTER 3

1. Target market refers to the group of people to whom you particularly want to market your services.

2. A financial analysis is critical to the success of the business development. It may prevent you from running out of money too soon in the project or as your business progresses.

3. Some of the most common body treatments offered in day spas are the salt glow rubs, full body algae and mud wraps, and herbal wraps.

4. It is vital to promote the hydrotherapy tub due to the large investment to buy it and in order to get your clients to want to utilize it fully.

5.   The advantage of offering packages is to give the client the opportunity to sample multiple services in one visit, and to let them feel like it's a mini destination spa visit.

CHAPTER 4

1.   Purchasing is complicated and confusing. The day spa owner can make a lot of mistakes if not careful.

2.   You must know why you want to open a day spa because if the motives are wrong, such as for a quick buck, you're choosing the wrong business. You must also know if you have the ability to make a go of it.

3.   A professional consultant may be the best dollar you ever spent. A professional can help prevent you from making mistakes, will help keep you organized, and guide you to suppliers along with being a great source for advice.

4.   High luxury market, upper middle market, middle market.

5.   Important factors to consider when choosing suppliers are credibility, delivery, education, service (any two are a correct answer).

6.   Beauty supply houses, esthetic distribution. Esthetic distribution.

7.   Considerations for choosing a product line are inequality of products, American versus European or imported, branded versus private label, support materials, retail/professional price structures, multiple lines, ingredients fads and trends, skin care versus makeup (any four are a correct answer).

8.   Considerations when purchasing equipment are construction, parts, training, support/service (any two are a correct answer).

9.   Accessories and supplies should certainly be programmed into your budget because they are necessary and also provide important cash income from sales.

CHAPTER 5

1.   Things that must be addressed in the business plan are introduction, mission statement, background, the new operation, management, management strength, competition, revenue projections, expense projections, loan request, assets, closing comments (any three are a correct answer).

CHAPTER 6

1.   There are many important points to consider in choosing the location including type of area, square footage, whether part of a mall or shopping center.

2. The square footage is very important because rent and many costs are based directly on the square footage of the property or area being discussed.

3. A few advantages of hiring an interior designer include to avoid disastrous mistakes, obtain professional advice, develop layouts, and save money.

4. Wet rooms.

5. It is not good to have the hydrotherapy tub and Vichy shower put in one room due to the American consumer's need for privacy, thus making the area's use confined to one person at a time when actually they could be used simultaneously if two rooms were available.

6. Wet rooms can be from about 9' × 12' to 12' × 14', the larger the better from a client's standpoint.

7. Even a massage room should have a sink from the standpoint of versatility, sanitation, and the ability to do some body treatments and rinse the client off.

8. Public areas include entry, reception, makeup, retail, offices, staff lounge, laundry, storage, bathrooms.

9. In a large, busy day spa, it is better to separate check-in and check-out areas to avoid overcrowding, noise that distracts the telephone receptionist, and to allow for the calm completion of retail sales.

10. Noise is an important factor in placing rooms in a day spa. It's wise to have the massage and facial rooms as far away from the noise as possible with hair or nails in the more open, talkative areas.

11. The owner should have an office in order to have a place to go to work or meet with staff.

12. Music can be a problem. There is a conflict between loud, bouncy music and quiet massage areas. The quiet areas need quiet music for relaxation.

13. Retail is the real income for the spa so plan for plenty of well-designed, well-lit retail areas.

14. State board of cosmetology, OSHA, Department of Health, Internal Revenue Service.

15. It's vital to investigate laws and regulations in advance of construction to avoid problems and costly mistakes.

CHAPTER 7

1. Major equipment should be ordered four to six weeks in advance of opening. If you are having something custom made you may need three to four months.

2. A computer system is imperative for a large spa and still useful for a small one in order to handle the accounting (revenue, expenses, etc.), inventory control, tracking client records, payroll, word processing, and scheduling.

3. A policies and procedures manual is a vital tool to help keep you organized and to help in staff management issues.

4. An employee evaluation is an organized method of constructively guiding the employee and improving on areas of weakness.

5. The most important reason to have an employee-based relationship is in order to have control over the management of your spa.

6. You should not advertise for a technician with a clientele because what you infer is that you really need the clientele. In addition, indirectly you are giving the employee permission to leave with your clients when he/she leaves you.

7. It's very important to cross-train employees in order to have a true team spirit and to fully utilize the capabilities of each.

8. The front desk person is important because he/she is the first impression a client has about your spa, and the impact can make or break the business.

9. The name of the salon should represent who you are and what you want to represent.

10. Packages are a natural sell in a day spa simply because the day spa represents an abbreviated version of what one might receive at a destination spa.

11. Your pricing may be determined by your actual cost per treatment, competition, experience, and what the potential client is willing to pay.

12. An appointment cancellation policy states in writing that if a client doesn't give twenty-four hours advance notification of cancellation, he/she is subject to being charged for the service.

13. Hours working career people need are early in the morning, late evenings, weekends including Sunday afternoons.

14. Yes, it's quite desirable to have shifts in the spa if you plan to have extended hours.

15. The official opening ceremony/celebration should not take place until all the bugs have been worked out of the new spa, at least a few weeks after a soft opening.

CHAPTER 8

1. We can point to the fact that beauty professionals are not good business people.

2. The definition of marketing is the act or process of selling or purchasing in a market; an aggregate of functions involved in moving goods from producer to consumer. The important words are, "aggregate of functions."

3. Paid advertising may include Yellow Pages, newspaper, television, radio, signs, billboards, magazines, local papers, donations.

4. The best form of advertising is word of mouth.

5. You should not give unlimited service donations because it costs money and requests may inundate you. You should determine a fixed budget for how many you're willing to give in a year.

6. A press release should be sent to the media at opening, when you add new services or products, when you receive an award or honor, when you attend seminars, anytime you can!

7. You are the best person to sell your business and by living and breathing it, you create potential clients in all of your contacts.

8. The two operative words in promotions are "plan" and "implement." Promotions won't happen just by thinking about them. You must logistically write out a plan, set dates, and then absolutely implement them. Keep the plan in mind ahead of time in order to facilitate proper execution of the plan.

9. It's a serious mistake to think we're above retailing. Retailing is not only the heart of the business but also our responsibility if we really care about that client and the home care program.

10. Retailing is a must for the day spa.

11. The staff must be knowledgeable to some degree in all departments in order to represent a professional image to the client and to maintain a cohesive team spirit.

12. It's important to value products at the retail value because our clients pay retail and the products are worth that price.

13. It's dangerous to book a technician back to back because it may kill the opportunity for the technician to make the retail sale. The spa loses income and the client loses the proper care.

14. A makeup display should be clean, freshly cleansed with sanitized brushes, mascara wands cut off, and disposable applicators available for the client to try products.

15. If you make your entire spa conducive to retail, the client should feel no need to go elsewhere for products.

CHAPTER 9

1. It's quite common for day spas to slack off after the first year perhaps due to fatigue or the mistaken feeling of having already "made it."

2. A good way to improve on your ordering procedures is to analyze your needs, project ahead, and order less often, ideally once a month. If you have a computer, you can also program it to produce an automatic order requisition when the inventory reaches a designated level.

3. Purchasing once a month will save you freight costs and may help you avail yourself of supplier discounts, free freight, "baker's dozens." It's a great money saver and can also amount to a lot of income.

4. Yes, it's possible to have so many lines that you have too much money tied up, lose control of inventory, and lose supplier responsibility for reactions.

5. Mail order from a day spa can generate a tremendous amount of income. It's a very wise thing to do.

6. A "mystery shopper" will visit your day spa and examine it with an outsider's objective opinion. This will help guide you in changes and improvements.

7. Employee apathy can be avoided by a number of things, some being your own excitement about the business, including them in decisions and plans, through meetings and events, and through advanced education.

8. Ongoing education is vital to stay on top of industry and technological trends. In particular, product knowledge updates are critical for the spa to increase income and proper client care.

9. The major problem associated with always trying to add "new things" is the frenzy that may be involved in maintaining it as the client begins to demand more and more.

10. It's a tremendous asset to have a number of advisers, from the ones you must pay for to the friends and experts in the industry you befriend.

APPENDIX
Industry Resources

ASSOCIATIONS

Aestheticians International Association, Inc. (AIA)
3939 E. Hwy 80 #408
Mesquite, TX 75150
(214) 686-2540

American Massage Therapy Association (AMTA)
820 Davis St. #100
Evanston, IL 60201-4444
(708) 864-0123

Associated Bodyworks and Massage Professionals
28677 Buffalo Park Rd.
Evergreen, CO 80439-8478
(303) 674-8478

International Spa and Fitness Association (I-Spa)
1300 L St., N.W. #1050
Washington, DC 20005
(202) 789-5920

CIDESCO USA SECTION is through membership in:
National Cosmetology Association (NCA)
3510 Olive St.
St. Louis, MO 63103
(314) 534-7980

(CIDESCO International Examinations may be taken through NCA or through CIDESCO Schools opening in the United States. CIDESCO represents the highest quality of esthetic achievement in the world and is recognized in more than thirty countries worldwide.)

MAGAZINES

Club Industry
Cardinal Business Media Inc.
1300 Virginia Dr. Ste. 400
Fort Washington, PA 19034
(708) 564-1385

Dermascope
3939 E. Hwy 80 #408
Mesquite, TX 75150
(214) 526-0752

Health & Beauty Salon
Reed Business Publishing Ltd.
Oakfield House
Haywards Heath
Sussex RH1633DH U.K.
01622-721666

Les Nouvelles Esthetiques, American Edition
306 Alcazar Ave. #204
Coral Gables, FL 33134
(305) 443-2322

Massage
Noah Publishing Company
P.O. Box 1500
Davis, CA 95617
(800) 872-1282

Modern Salon
Vance Publishing Co.
P.O. Box 1414
Lincolnshire, IL 60069
(800) 621-2845

SalonNews
P.O. Box 5035
Brentwood, TN 37024-5035
(800) 477-6411

SalonOvations
P.O. Box 12519
Albany, NY 12212-2519
(914) 368-4146

Salon Technologies
8551 N.W. 10th St.
Pembroke Pines, FL 33024
(305) 437-4580

Skin, Inc.
Allured Publishing
362 S. Schmale Rd.
Carol Stream, IL 60188-2787
(708) 653-2155

Bibliography

B.D.I.T., Inc. Spas. *The International Spa Guide*. Port Washington, N.Y.: B.D.I.T., Inc., 1990.

The Burton Goldberg Group. *Alternative Medicine, The Definitive Guide*. Puyallup, Wash.: Future Medicine Publishing, Inc., 1994.

Gerson, Joel. *Milady's Standard Textbook for Professional Estheticians*. Albany, N.Y.: Milady Publishing Company, A Division of Delmar Publishers Inc., 1992.

Hirsch, Judith Brode. *The Spa Book*. New York: Spa Resources, Perigee Books, The Putnam Publishing Group, 1988.

Joseph, Jeffrey with Dari Giles. *Spa Finders' Guide to Spa Vacations at Home and Abroad*. New York: Philip Lief Group, Inc., John Wiley & Sons, 1990.

Lees, Mark. *Milady's Skin Care Reference Guide*. Albany, N.Y.: Milady Publishing Company, A Division of Delmar Publishers Inc., 1994.

Michalun, Natalia and M. Varinia Michalun. *Skin Care and Cosmetic Ingredients Dictionary*. Albany, N.Y.: Milady Publishing Company, A Division of Delmar Publishers Inc., 1994.

Phillips, Carole. *SalonOvations: It's In the Bag; Selling in the Salon*. Albany, N.Y.: Milady Publishing Company, A Division of Delmar Publishers Inc., 1995.

Van Itallie, Theodore B., M.D. and Leila Hadley. *The Best of Spas*. New York: Harper & Row, 1988.

Glossary/Index

Notes

Notes

Notes

Notes

Style.
Savvy.
Solutions.

every month.
SalonOvations

SalonOvations is a professional and personal magazine designed with you in mind. Each issue delivers great features on personal growth and on-target stories about the beauty business. Get helpful hints from industry pros on starting your own salon business and how to satisfy your clients. Plus, you'll get pages of colorful photos of the latest trends in haircutting, styling and coloring.

All this at a great price of ~~12~~ **15** issues for only $19.95 a year! **3 FREE issues** - Save over 40% (price subject to change)